CHARLOTTE BEDFORD

MAKING WAVES BEHIND BARS

The Prison Radio Association

First published in Great Britain in 2018 by

Bristol University Press
University of Bristol
1-9 Old Park Hill
Bristol
BS2 8BB
UK
t: +44 (0)117 954 5940
www.bristoluniversitypress.co.uk

North America office:
Bristol University Press
c/o The University of Chicago Press
1427 East 60th Street
Chicago, IL 60637, USA
t: +1 773 702 7700
f: +1 773 702 9756
sales@press.uchicago.edu
www.press.uchicago.edu

© Bristol University Press 2018

British Library Cataloguing in Publication Data
A catalogue record for this book is available from the British Library.

Library of Congress Cataloging-in-Publication Data
A catalog record for this book has been requested.

ISBN 978-1-5292-0336-3 (hardback)
ISBN 978-1-5292-0343-1 (ePub)
ISBN 978-1-5292-0345-5 (Mobi)
ISBN 978-1-5292-0338-7 (ePDF)

The right of Charlotte Bedford to be identified as author of this work has been asserted by her in accordance with the Copyright, Designs and Patents Act 1988.

All rights reserved: no part of this publication may be reproduced, stored in a retrieval system, or transmitted in any form or by any means, electronic, mechanical, photocopying, recording, or otherwise without the prior permission of Bristol University Press.

Every reasonable effort has been made to obtain permission to reproduce copyrighted material. If, however, anyone knows of an oversight, please contact the publisher.

The statements and opinions contained within this publication are solely those of the author and not of the University of Bristol or Bristol University Press. The University of Bristol and Bristol University Press disclaim responsibility for any injury to persons or property resulting from any material published in this publication.

Bristol University Press works to counter discrimination on grounds of gender, race, disability, age and sexuality.

Cover design by blu inc, Bristol
Front cover: image kindly supplied by Arthur Hagues
Printed and bound in Great Britain by CPI Group (UK) Ltd, Croydon, CR0 4YY
Bristol University Press uses environmentally responsible print partners

Contents

Acknowledgements		iv
Foreword		v
Introduction		1
Part I	**A Framework For Understanding Prison Radio**	**17**
1	'The Power of Radio': Radio and Social Change	19
2	'Making Waves Behind Bars': The Prison Context	39
3	'Making a Difference': Social Action and Enterprise	59
Part II	**Prison Radio Association Case Studies**	**79**
4	Rethinking Public Service Broadcasting: the PRA and the BBC	81
5	Transformative Prison Education: The Prison Radio Training Project	101
6	Changing the Prison Narrative: The PRA and News Media	121
7	Restorative Justice in Action: The *Face to Face* Documentary	141
Part III	**Conclusions**	**161**
8	Ten Years On: Global Themes in Prison Radio Development	163
References		177
Index		189

Acknowledgements

First and foremost, I am indebted to the prison radio practitioners who gave me the trust and freedom to carry out this research. This debt extends to the inspiration, strength and commitment of many of the people I have met along the way, including prisoners, prison staff, and those who continue to work tirelessly to support prisoners and their families. I am grateful to Tim Wall for believing in my academic endeavours, and to my partner in prisoner radio research and practice, Heather Anderson, for encouraging me to write the book. I also acknowledge the support of the University of Adelaide in the process. And finally, I thank my incredibly patient family for continuing to support my work and indulging my musings and ranting.

Foreword

Prison is lonely. Not without a sense of irony, I remember sitting in my cell with hundreds of people within a few dozen yards of me – and yet I had seldom felt more alone. Instead of a name, I had been given a number to use when required to interact with the institution for anything of any tangible significance. I had essentially been stripped of individuality. My peers and I were a mass of criminals and no sense of what might lie beyond the walls could be found by staring at the many nameless reflections I co-inhabited with. But I wasn't, and am never going to be, a totality of my offences. Nor would my neighbour – or his! This conflict of knowing you should be more is painful when you struggle to see *how*.

So, how do we find humanity in a place like this? To know that you are not alone, to know that someone else feels like you, is a basis on which you can begin to imagine yourself somewhere else. For me, this came in the form of the *Rock Show* on National Prison Radio (NPR). Through so many different stages of my life, the one constant has been my passion for metal. It was a 'normal', pro-social point of connection with people – the sort of thing most people would talk about with their friends. But discussing the latest band seemed to mean more to me at times when I could find very few reasons to keep trying. Writing in to the *Rock Show*, knowing there were other people going through the relative ups and downs that I was, and having a platform in which to explore those things was – sometimes – the only thing I could look forward to.

The weekly show runs for two hours a time and was repeated on a Saturday evening. The other 164 hours felt like an eternity. I was stuck in my cell and my head for most of that. A conversation began between a guy on the other side of the country and myself. It took months to finish. We were suggesting our favourite drummer. Obviously, this didn't matter. Obviously, we had long sentences to serve, people we had hurt and families we had left behind ... and obviously I was right. But it was precisely because it didn't matter, that the weight of our lives, for those few moments felt manageable and – almost – trivial, that the following week felt surmountable.

NPR softened the severity just enough for me to think I could do something about it. It came, too, with advice about prison life that genuinely helped: what to do if you want to sort your addiction out; what happens if things are getting on top of you; and stories of people who had come through it. It never let me forget about what I had to do, but it made me feel like there were so many more reasons to do it than I had first thought.

This book gives insight into the growth of prison radio initiatives and, in particular, the birth of the Prison Radio Association. The Prison Radio Association begins to challenge our thoughts on what an offender *is*. The ever-increasing range of programmes reflects how complex individuals are. By providing insight into who makes up our prison population, and using this to understand what sorts of help people need, the PRA reach out to those in debt-crisis, coping with grief, conflicted by identity, cultural or religious difficulties. For ten years, now, there has been a developing and reflexive platform which does not assume who criminals are. It has asked them who they are. And, in turn, this research sheds light on what prison radio can do and does. I am convinced that NPR, and the *Rock Show*, saved my life. I am sure that, if this is the case, I am not the only person it has saved.

Gareth Evans
Criminology Student at Anglia Ruskin University
National Prison Radio fan!

Introduction

Radio produced and broadcast behind prison walls is a unique response to the increasing global incarceration crisis, able to support people through their sentences, improve prison communications, and address the causes of recidivism through access to information. In the first study to explore the growth of radio stations in prisons, this book examines the early history of the Prison Radio Association (PRA) in the United Kingdom, the first organisation of its kind in the world. Established in 2006 to network and support individual prison radio projects, the PRA created the world's first National Prison Radio service within two years. A decade later and the organisation continues to manage and develop National Prison Radio; has established an award-winning production company; is creating media services for people on release from prison; and advises emerging prison radio stations internationally.

Focusing on the initial development of the PRA and National Prison Radio (NPR), this work examines the process through which relatively small-scale media activism, based on prisoners' rights, came to be an intrinsic part of prison culture in the UK, playing a central role in institutional operations. It considers prison radio growth within the context of political and economic change, and argues that the successful development of an independent, prisoner-led service represents resistance against the forces of corporatisation and managerialism that have redefined the organisation and function of broadcasting, punishment and social welfare. Against a backdrop of public service privatisation and media commercialisation, the growth of the PRA illustrates the complex processes of working in partnership with institutions and agencies to give a voice to people in prison. It is a story which highlights the enduring importance of social values in broadcasting, represents new opportunities for social activism, and presents radio as a powerful force for social change.

Prison radio has emerged from a contradictory media landscape characterised by the concentration of global commercial media power on the one hand, and the democratisation and expansion of non-mainstream media on the other. As Mitzi Waltz argues, where mainstream media is shaped by corporate power, it has 'never been less trusted by its readers and viewers' (2005, p.1). The situation has led to an increase in non-mainstream, alternative and activist media in which radio plays a prominent role, building on a strong history of independent activism.

Radio is undergoing a dramatic transformation shaped by developments in digital technology and redefined in the era of participatory media. As media institutions struggle to justify their positions in the face of a seemingly endless array of diverse platforms and content, radio has risen to the challenge most successfully through digital radio and online formats. It remains relatively affordable to make, transmit and listen to, contributing to its enduring status as the most pervasive and democratic media worldwide (Hendy 2000), able to reach the most geographically and socially isolated locations in society (Tacchi 2000), including prisons.

Similarly, the prison context is a shifting and controversial landscape. Debate on crime and punishment has become increasingly politicised over recent decades, with prisons becoming more visible than ever through a proliferation of mass media crime-related news, television dramas and reality shows. Yet prison remains a mysterious and mythologised space, represented through a simplified discourse of danger that fails to ask questions around prisoner treatment, prisoner rights and whether prison even works as a solution to crime. The role of prison is widely recognised as suffering from ongoing and deepening crisis (Sim 2009), failing to address the problems of crime and crime control in society. As French sociologist Loïc Wacquant so eloquently argues, 'We must theorise the prison not as a technical implement of law enforcement, but as a core political capacity whose selective and aggressive deployment in the lower regions of social space violates the ideals of democratic citizenship' (2010, p.197).

In the UK, outdated and inadequate facilities and rapidly increasing prisoner numbers have impacted on institutional operations, while a process of privatisation and spread of managerialism have contributed to a crisis of legitimacy, raising questions about the function and efficacy of current approaches to crime and punishment and leading to a seemingly constant stream of interventions to address the problems faced. Again, the landscape is one of contradictions, characterised by increasingly punitive political discourse and policy reform on the one hand, and a language of rehabilitation that has come to shape criminal justice practice on the other. Where radio is concerned with communication and information, prison remains an isolated and misunderstood space. This book examines the ways in which such contrasting and disparate arenas meet, and considers the implications for the changing meanings of both.

PRA beginnings

Before detailing the focus and structure of the research, an overview of the PRA story serves to clarify what is meant by prison radio in this context and sets the scene for the following analysis:

> 'About 70 or 80 boys arrive each day in big buses. You are stripped, given a number, a box of clothes. You are put in a large room with 60 other boys, big guys staring at you. There's a lot of friction when you arrive and you've got to front it out. If you sit in a corner with your head down they will pick on you for sure ... if you show fear your card is marked. I've seen guys with fear in their eyes ... you get smashed around the head, sent to hospital and

you're back on the wing the same night ... Some of the boys are so frightened they won't come out of their cells.' (Sim 1994, p.104)

This prisoner account provides a vivid description of the systemic culture of violence within Her Majesty's Young Offender Institution (HMYOI) Feltham, West London, in March 1992. Four prisoners had died by suicide in the preceding seven months, and an additional 40 prisoners were attempting to end their own lives each month amid what Joe Sim describes as an 'atmosphere of terror' (1994, p.104).

When asked where the idea for prison radio came from, PRA co-founder, Mark Robinson (2012), refers to the media coverage of high suicide and self-injury rates at the prison, which was close to where he lived. He talks of his chance involvement with hospital radio fundraising at the time, and of having the idea that prison radio could work in much the same way, helping to keep prisoners company when they were at their most vulnerable in their cells alone at night. After gaining the enthusiastic support of the prison governor, who was all too happy to take on any new ideas and support to address the problems faced, Mark Robinson enlisted the help of his friend and neighbour, Roma Hooper. When asked to reflect on her first engagement with prison radio, she recalls the summer afternoon that he knocked on her door to ask for help with fundraising. She describes prisons as not having been "on my radar at all" and, after visiting HMYOI Feltham, talks of being struck by the realisation that the prisoners were "just children" (Hooper, 2012). They were locked up for extended periods with little or no human contact, and limited access to activities or even television – from Hooper's perspective, radio was a clear way for children in custody to maintain contact with the outside world.

Fast forward to 2006, and a large room in the education block of Her Majesty's Prison (HMP) Birmingham, an imposing Victorian built local prison housing almost 1,500 adult remand

and sentenced male prisoners. The room was filled with managers from prisons around the country together with senior representatives from criminal justice agencies, non-profit and education sector organisations, and the BBC. For the majority of the media and external agency representatives, it was the first time they had visited a prison, leaving mobile telephones behind, experiencing the complex security procedures of entering the airlock doors, being searched, and waiting patiently while the many gates were unlocked and locked on the slow transit through the building. Guests were gathered for the official launch of the Prison Radio Association and to hear about the work of a pilot project run in partnership with the BBC.

The accompanying CD, *Making Waves Behind Bars,* showcases audio produced by and with people serving time in three prisons in the West Midlands region. It includes a range of features addressing the question *Does Prison Work?,* the experience of being *Inside at Christmas,* and a story on *The Family Man,* a play written and performed by prisoners working with the group, *Safe Ground* (PRA 2006). When asked to reflect on the development of the PRA, Chief Executive Phil Maguire (2012) describes the project as a major turning point for prison radio, moving from "lads spinning records and doing shout-outs to their friends", to a focus on speech-based content, "it became about offering an innovative way of drawing educationally hard to reach prisoners back into the classroom".

In November of the following year, visitors were assembled for a similar event in a room at HMP Brixton in London. This time, a range of high profile figures attended the launch of the PRA's flagship radio station, Electric Radio Brixton, including representatives from the newly formed Ministry of Justice, recently restructured National Offender Management Service, and musicians Billy Bragg and Mick Jones on behalf of their charity, Jail Guitar Doors. It was here that Phil Maguire first pitched the next major stage of development for the PRA, the idea of a national prison radio service. From a focus on working with small groups of prisoners to make radio, Electric Radio Brixton demonstrated the potential for programming to impact not only on the lives of the HMP Brixton audience, but the entire prison population of England and Wales.

National Prison Radio

The vision was realised less than two years after the original pitch, with Electric Radio Brixton relaunched as National Prison Radio in 2009. NPR now broadcasts as an audio channel through in-cell televisions in over 100 prisons, reaching a potential audience of around 80,000 people at any time. The service provides music and speech programming for 24 hours a day, seven days a week, allowing listeners to tune in to a designated television channel whenever they choose. Radios, CD players and even written materials in prisons are often restricted to those who can pay for them. An audio service through television sets ensures as wide an access as possible when people are in their cells. This widespread availability has additional relevance during the reception, induction and settling in period at a new prison when people are particularly isolated, need to learn about prison processes, and their money allowances and work allocations are yet to be set up.

The service was launched and rolled out in partnership with the Ministry of Justice through the National Offender Management Service (NOMS), the government agency responsible for running prisons. Following a 2017 restructure, responsibility for prisons and probation services now falls within the remit of Her Majesty's Prison and Probation Service (HMPPS) which continues to work closely with the PRA, recognising the importance of NPR for increasing communication and linking people to support services. Through previous roles with NOMS, HMPPS Chief Executive Officer Michael Spurr has supported NPR from the outset, commenting that, 'The success of NPR continues to amaze. The quality of the work remains excellent and the benefits huge. We are lucky to have such professional and committed partners doing such a great job' (PRA 2017b).

The partnership is facilitated through the role of a dedicated HMPPS Head of Prison Radio, seconded from the BBC and responsible for liaising with the PRA to maintain and develop NPR. A decade into the arrangement and much of the current focus is around strategies to upgrade the existing broadcast infrastructure in line with changes in technology to ensure that each prison has unbroken access to the service. In 2009, the Ministry of Justice began investing in the equipment and installation for each prison to receive and transmit NPR. All content is pre-recorded, and each hour of programming is scheduled at HMP Brixton using a standard radio automation software linked to an external server and sent to a specialist broadcast company. The signal is then sent to a satellite, and beamed across the UK, Europe and North Africa before being picked up by a satellite dish on the roof of the prison. A dedicated NPR computer in each prison then links the service to the in-cell television network. Within ten years, what was once a straightforward and cost-effective offer is now becoming outdated and unreliable, and moving NPR to a digital service has become a practical and viable option.

NPR is made by and for prisoners, heard only behind the prison walls. It is designed to support prisoners through their sentences and aims to reduce reoffending by providing information and support to help people rebuild their lives in preparation for release. As with any other radio service, programming is driven by the needs and responses of its audience. Examples include the breakfast show, *Porridge*. Following the standard format, it combines music and talk, but presented by prisoners talking about topical subjects that are relevant to a specific audience. It aims to provide a positive soundtrack to the start of the prison day and helps to create a feeling of community, receiving a nomination for 'Breakfast Show of the Year' at the prestigious radio industry Sony Radio Academy Awards in 2012.

The Request Show has become the cornerstone of programming and is by far the most successful show for encouraging audience contact. Again, it builds a sense of community by being a friendly and human voice in an environment that can be isolating and aggressive. In 2016, NPR received 6,641 letters from prisoners and 3,878 requests and letters of support from prisoners' friends and loved ones, demonstrating the degree of listener engagement and providing a vital means of contact, communication and connection (PRA 2017b):

> 'NPR has given me the confidence to write to people and I have now made contact with many people on the outside … NPR affects the lives of every listener.' (NPR Listener, HMYOI Lancaster Farms)

NPR programming is primarily made at two production hubs, HMP Brixton, a men's training and resettlement prison in London, and HMP Styal, a women's prison in Cheshire. Not only do the two centres increase the range of regional accents that listeners will relate to, but the balance ensures the representation of women's voices within the prison system. The incarceration of women in England and Wales has escalated dramatically in the past decade, and is currently among the highest in Western Europe. Yet in representing only 5% of the overall prison population, women hold a minority status which means they are easily overlooked in policy, planning and services, often treated as 'correctional afterthoughts' (Prison Reform Trust 2017b).

Effective radio needs to be relevant and viewed as credible by its target audience. Far from being a 'captive audience', prisoners have the power to turn off at any time. Prisoner participation in NPR programming is critical for engaging listeners and creating a sense of ownership and investment in the service. Programming is developed, produced and presented by prisoners working alongside small teams of professional radio producers based in

HMPs Brixton and Styal. To ensure programming is as diverse and representative as possible, the NPR team visits two prisons each month to record a 'Takeover Day'. NPR producers work with prisoners to choose music and record interviews, discussion and shout-outs, producing all of station's main programme strands across the day from a different prison.

Participation is equally important for the NPR aim of reducing reoffending. People with lived experience of prison are the experts on the strategies that work, a role that has long been promoted by prisoner advocacy groups and is increasingly acknowledged by service providers and policy makers. This shift is highlighted by social worker, Claire Seppings, whose study of over 60 reintegration models in the UK, US, Republic of Ireland and Sweden (2015) demonstrates the impact of involving former prisoners in peer mentoring programmes. The role of the 'expert citizen' is central to the relevance and credibility of prison radio – who better to talk about the issues that matter to prisoners than the people who have experienced it themselves? As the induction booklet for new NPR station workers states, 'Your listeners share your experience of being in prison. You know as well as they do what prison is like. You know what the challenges are' (PRA 2016b).

The NPR programme schedule is updated regularly, able to respond to listener feedback and build on the skills and specialist music knowledge of the prisoner producers working in the team at any point. Regular programmes include *Sound Women*, the HMP Styal take on the longstanding BBC Radio Four *Woman's Hour*, and *Outside In,* providing practical advice and support for people coming to the end of their sentences. Awareness of NPR throughout the criminal justice sector has steadily grown, leading to an increasing number of partnerships and commissions which not only represent an important income source for the PRA, but helps to address the needs of specific groups of listeners. Programmes include *Roll Call* for people who have spent time in the armed services, *Open Road* for the

Gypsy, Roma and Traveller community, and *Safe*, a programme for those who have spent time in the care system. *Safe* recognises the over-representation of care leavers in the criminal justice system and raise awareness of available support. Over 25% of the adult prison population has previously been in care (Berman and Dar 2013), a figure even more significant given that children in care and care leavers account for less than 1% of the general population (The Care Leavers Association 2013).

Research focus and structure

The PRA has developed its services, audience and reputation at a rate that comparative independent media projects have struggled to achieve. From the launch of the PRA in 2006 to the roll-out of a national service in 2009, the rapid pace of change is strikingly apparent. It is this period of intense growth which is the focus of the following chapters. It is also a period which the author was involved as a prison radio practitioner, a position which has shaped the design and direction of the research.

Through my role as regional manager for a national media training charity, I was approached to bring an education focus to the original West Midlands prison radio pilot project in 2005. As the PRA became established, I moved into the organisation's second staff role, employed as Education Director to manage a two-year training pilot before a planned move to Australia. I have worked and volunteered in community radio since the early 1980s and continue to be inspired by the role radio can play in giving a voice to the most excluded and misrepresented people in society. My experience as a member of the founding PRA team remains the most prominent example of this. After immigrating, I observed the relationship between radio and prisons within a dramatically different setting and soon became aware of the vast array of diverse factors involved in the PRA story. As a result, I set out to examine the factors involved in the story of UK prison radio, and to use my research background to understand the possibilities of replicating and adapting future models.

Radio produced for and by prisoners is a growing field of practice and research worldwide. Activity has evolved through different models, broadly divided into two intersecting formats: programmes produced inside prison for a prison audience, and those produced outside, primarily aimed at a prison audience. A range of radio services, stations, programmes and podcast series are currently operating in countries including the US, Australia, Canada, Poland, Israel, Hungary, Sweden, Norway, Ecuador, El Salvador, and Trinidad and Tobago. Each has developed in a different format to meet the needs and challenges of prison populations in different locations, shaped by the opportunities and restrictions within different correctional systems at a particular time. Therefore, no single model can provide a blueprint for prison radio. Instead, I set out to investigate the unique contexts and conditions that led to the growth of the PRA and launch of NPR. The examination of the motivations, challenges and strategies involved in the process provides a useful case study to inform the development of a growing global movement of prison radio, highlighting the broader ways in which emerging media practices are being used to affect social change.

To this end, the research draws primarily on the reflective accounts of the people involved in the early stages of prison radio development, including the volunteer founders of Radio Feltham and the key players responsible for establishing the PRA, Electric Radio Brixton and National Prison Radio. This does not extend to the perspectives of the prisoners involved, work which would have been structured around the unique ethical and practical considerations of research in prisons. Instead, the aim is to understand the motivations and experiences of those driven to change the lives of prisoners from the outside.

During a research trip to the UK in 2012, interviews were carried out with participants who played an instrumental role in the launch of the PRA and NPR. While the sample population is relatively small, it is representative of both the PRA as a growing organisation, and prison radio activity as a whole. In recognition of this, attention was paid to securing a range of perspectives by talking to representatives from different aspects of prison radio, including training, operations, content production, and prison management.

- Roma Hooper – PRA Chair and Co-founder
- Mark Robinson – PRA Secretary and Co-founder
- Phil Maguire – PRA Chief Executive and former BBC Prison Radio Co-ordinator
- Andrew Wilkie – PRA Director of Radio and Operations and former Electric Radio Brixton Station Manager
- Kieron Tilley – PRA Trustee and former inaugural PRA Chair and PRA Director of Operations
- Paul McDowell – PRA Trustee and former Governor of HMP Brixton, Chief Executive of NACRO (at time of interview) and HM Chief Inspector of Probation
- Jules McCarthy – Senior Lecturer in Broadcast Journalism, Staffordshire University and former PRA Project Co-ordinator

The themes identified within the interviews led to the exploration of secondary texts including newspaper stories, policy documents and radio content. The examination of participant accounts as discursive and representational practices draws on Michel Foucault's notion of discourse as that which constructs knowledge and meaning (2002). As Stuart Hall suggests, discourse 'governs the way that a topic can be meaningfully talked about and reasoned about' (1997, p.15). Consequently, meaning is transient, fixed only by discursive and representational practices at a particular moment (Mason 2006, p.253).

A focus on discourse in both theory and method has shaped the research process, recognising that the ways in which PRA founders and practitioners reflect on their experiences and make sense of what they do defines the activity. In addition, analysis of newspaper coverage of prison radio-related issues at the time, and a later National Prison Radio programme, considers prison radio as regime of representation, contributing to wider discourse on imprisonment which creates new meanings around prison and prisoners. As Paul Mason demonstrates, it is an approach which recognises that 'while objects exist outside of discourse, it is only through discourse that knowledge and meaning are produced' (2006, p.253).

The following chapters are divided into two sections. Part I presents an analysis of the existing ideas that can be used to shed light on the subject of radio in prisons. Starting with a focus on radio, I relate prison radio growth to dramatic changes in the ways in which broadcasting, prisons and social activism are organised and conceptualised, and argue that the development of an independent, prisoner-led service represents resistance against the managerial and economic rationalities which have redefined all three arenas. First, the PRA belief in the transformative 'power of radio' provides a starting point from which to examine the broadcast context. Chapter One considers the complex historical relationship between government, radio and social change. In particular, this highlights the unique positioning of prison radio, relating at once to alternative, grassroots media to empower a misrepresented group, and to the changing institutional role and function of public service broadcasting.

Attention then turns to the penal context in which neoliberal rationalities and technologies have transformed the role and function of prisons. NPR is considered as a product of the prison industrial complex while equally representing resistance against punitive individualised responses to crime control, placing those with lived prison experience at the centre of discussion on potential ways to reduce imprisonment. Finally, the growth of the PRA is mapped against shifts in social policy reform which have redefined and repositioned the role of the non-profit sector. Theories of volunteerism and social activism frame the discussion of early, informal activity while the formal establishment of the PRA demonstrates the merging of these themes with the rise of social enterprise and entrepreneurship.

This discussion provides a framework for Part II, which focuses on the two most prominent themes identified throughout the accounts of PRA participants:

- the partnerships and institutional arrangements involved in the process; and
- the management of perceptions and assumptions about prison radio which have influenced the process.

Two key partnership projects are identified as launching and shaping the PRA in the earliest stages. First, the role of the BBC is examined in facilitating a regional prison radio pilot project that led to the formalisation of the PRA. This is followed by discussion of a prison radio education project run in partnership with a range of prisons, state agencies, non-profit organisations, and broadcast institutions. The examples illustrate the neoliberal reworking of social welfare provision achieved through a focus on intersectoral partnerships. This context highlights the importance of maintaining organisational independence in order to develop a service which prioritises prisoner engagement and agency.

Building on the theme of managing institutional relationships, the following chapters focus on the ways in which PRA founders responded to negative perceptions and assumptions about the prison radio concept as the activity developed. Again, two key examples are used to illustrate the challenges faced. An analysis of mainstream print media coverage of stories relating to prison radio shows the ways in which the PRA developed and managed a media strategy to reduce reputational risk. This is followed by discussion of a 2012 NPR restorative justice radio documentary, which indicates a shift in the wider acceptance and legitimacy of prison radio.

Having outlined the context, causes and challenges behind the development of the PRA and launch of the world's first national prison radio service in 2009, the concluding chapter explores the significance of prison radio ten years on, highlighting the potential for development internationally.

In the first study to document the growth of UK prison radio, tell the stories of those involved, and bring together a body of references to assist further research, the recollections of PRA participants illustrate the complex processes through which grassroots media activism grew to be a recognised and established part of prison culture. The success of the PRA model lies in independence and the ability to balance dual, seemingly contradictory, functions linked to prison management and state control, while simultaneously remaining based in social activism, empowering prisoners with a voice.

PART I

A Framework For Understanding Prison Radio

1

'The Power of Radio': Radio and Social Change

The Prison Radio Association (PRA) states its core aim as contributing to the reduction of reoffending through 'the power of radio' (PRA 2017a). I use this statement as a starting point from which to explore the key ideas around radio as a socially and individually transformative medium in order to inform the understanding of how it came to be used in prison. Through discussion of existing literature, this chapter outlines the shifting relationship between radio broadcasting and social change and argues that the evolution and establishment of radio within prisons is indicative of new opportunities for media activism, demonstrating the enduring social relevance and impact of radio.

The unique position of prison radio is a central theme throughout this study, relating at once to institutional and governmental roles while equally framed in a commitment to prisoners' rights. In later chapters I outline key developmental stages in the PRA story, demonstrating the extent to which prison radio discourse and practice remains rooted in social activism and highlighting the importance of organisational independence in the process. In this chapter, I place the development of National Prison Radio within a wider debate on the history and future of non-commercial broadcasting, based on the balance between governmental regulation and control on the one hand and the countercultural opportunities it produces on the other.

As prison radio is a non-profit, socially-motivated media that focuses on the voices, representations and empowerment of a marginalised and disenfranchised group, the understanding of it is informed by discussion of alternative, activist, citizens', and community radio theory. In addition, partnership working with both the Prison Service and the BBC connects the development of the PRA to the changing role and function of institutional, mainstream media. Developing through the late 1990s and early 2000s in the UK, the convergence of two themes within the non-commercial media sector impacted on the establishment of the PRA:

- An increasingly regulated, formalised and professionalised community radio sector, repositioned as a public service with a specified community development remit.
- An increasingly deregulated, managerialised and marketised public service broadcasting (PSB) sector, struggling to redefine and justify its role through a reinvigorated focus on community engagement.

As a relatively new field of research and practice, there are limited studies that explicitly address the use of radio in prisons, yet the role radio can play in reconnecting prisoners with civil society is a prominent theme throughout. Heather Anderson (2012) provides the most thorough analysis to date, presenting an international inventory of community radio programming for prisoners, together with detailed case studies from Australia and Canada. Programmes made outside the prison are broadcast for a prisoner audience with content ranging from song requests to discussion on criminal justice issues. As Anderson shows, engaging with radio through listening, writing letters and, in some cases, presenting shows on release, plays an important part in maintaining family and community links, becoming a means through which prisoners enact citizenship and reconnect with notions of civic responsibility.

The communication environment

Before examining the historic and ongoing connection between radio and notions of democracy and civic participation, it is worth considering the unique communication environment of the prison. As well as structures of physical separation, prisons are spaces of information isolation. Mobile telephones are strictly banned, newspapers are a luxury, telephone calls are restricted and costly, television and radio sets are an earned incentive for good behaviour, and efforts to introduce controlled internet use have only just begun. The restriction of prisoner access to means of communication with the outside world may seem obvious. Yet as Anderson argues, maintaining contact and retaining some sense of membership with society are vital for successful reintegration (2012, p.223).

The introduction of media technologies into the prison environment challenges the historical meanings and functions of the archetypal closed institution, whether radio programming, access to telephones on the wings (Prison Reform Trust 2013) or televisions in cells (Knight 2015). As Foucault (1991) describes, the origins of the contemporary mass incarceration system lie in the belief that separation, solitude and quiet contemplation lead to moral reform. Deprivation and isolation represent a continuation of 18th century penal philosophies which have no relevance in the modern age, where communication and connection are recognised as central to building social cohesion (Jewkes and Johnston 2009).

When considering the extent that communication technologies have transformed the ways in which we work, learn and socialise, depriving prisoners of the tools and skills with which to engage with society creates a digital disadvantage which inhibits rehabilitation. Making the case for increasing computer and internet access in prisons, Yvonne Jewkes and Helen Johnston connect communications rights with social inclusion and argue that, where digital technologies have revolutionised everyday life, access becomes 'a basic right of citizenship' (2009, p.132).

Limited and controlled access to computer technology and secure web content has been adopted in pockets of activity across Europe, the UK and the US, recognised as valuable for enabling prisoners to stay in touch with families and obtain services and support, such as housing, education and employment, to help them desist from crime (Prison Reform Trust 2013). Nick Hardwick, Chair of the Parole Board for England and Wales and former Her Majesty's Chief Inspector of Prisons, calls for drastic change, describing the prison estate as wallowing in a 'pre-internet dark age, leaving prisoners woefully unprepared for the real world they will face on release' (Prison Reform Trust 2013). Yet progress is slow due to the challenges of developing a coordinated strategy to such fast-moving technologies and continually thwarted by perceived risks around security, criminal activity and offending victims (Tighe 2016).

When asked to consider 'why radio?' PRA Chief Executive Phil Maguire describes it as an intensely personal medium, one which people instinctively understand (2012). Radio is at once ubiquitous and invisible (Lewis and Booth 1989). This taken-for-granted nature contributes to its ability to 'fly under the radar' in comparison to the perceived dangers of computer and internet technologies in prison. Radio theorist Peter Lewis (2000) bemoans the low cultural status of sound and radio, highlighting a gap between private experience and public status. He argues that the private, intimate nature of radio has resulted in it becoming a 'secret pleasure' that needs no explanation or discussion in the public sphere, 'the intimate things it does for us as a friend, trusted informant and soundtrack for living, are almost literally unmentionable in public' (Lewis, 2000, p.161). While the description may seem emotive, these private and personal qualities are particularly useful for understanding its relevance and impact for prisoners.

Prison is noisy, crowded, impersonal and intimidating, and prisoners are not only isolated in the physical sense, but through separation from family and support networks, and often through the barriers they create as a form of self-preservation. Where emotional support is limited, the 'trusted friend' status of radio is able to offer comfort, raise morale and provide a sense of stability. Unlike other media forms, radio engages our imaginations helping us to construct pictures of the world, our communities and our place within them (Douglas 2004). In her examination of the role of radio in shaping American culture, Susan J. Douglas makes valuable observations on radio listening, highlighting the do-it-yourself nature and the mental activity involved (2004, p.4). These factors contribute to the ability to retain or alter mood, and to be emotionally evocative and reassuring (Tacchi 2000). In the contemporary media environment, people still turn to radio to alter or sustain particular emotional states, 'even as mere background noise, radio provides people with a sense of security that silence does not, which is why they actively turn to it, even if they aren't actively listening' (Douglas 2004, p.8).

In-cell television is now an established feature within UK prisons, acknowledged for providing resources for education, information and entertainment as well as preserving a sense of self and retaining connections with families and communities (Jewkes and Johnston 2009; Knight 2015). Victoria Knight highlights the anxiety and trepidation that marked the original roll-out, linked to public fears perpetuated through popular media (2015). At the core of this is a fundamental contradiction. Where policy makers and prison managers support the development of communication technologies as a means of reducing operational costs, the same stakeholders are 'mindful almost to the point of paranoia' about the risk of access being perceived as privilege and incurring the wrath of the popular press (Jewkes and Reisdorf 2016, p.535).

As discussed in later chapters, the same theme is prominent throughout the PRA story. To a large extent, the ways in which the organisation was able to successfully navigate the process can be attributed to the unique qualities of the radio medium, representing a relatively non-threatening and low-cost middle ground for increasing access to information and communication in contrast to the colossal and nebulous task of coordinating internet access. Knight connects fear around prisoner access to communicative technologies to the degree of user engagement involved, distinguishing it from television and radio, 'what this fundamentally means in the context of the prison is that the prisoner can 'reach' the outside world and the world can also reach them' (Knight, 2015, p.2). However, Knight's comments focus on the traditional one-way function of broadcasting, an assumption which fails to acknowledge the two-way qualities of radio which are central to the development and success of the NPR model, where listener feedback and prisoner participation are prioritised. This position needs further examination, firstly through establishing the democratic credentials of radio within a dramatically shifting mediascape, followed by the ways in which these features have played out historically.

Radio democracy

Radio is undergoing a dramatic transformation in the digital era, redefined through the growth of online distribution and increasing affordability of production technology. In a rapidly changing mediascape where consumers have seemingly limitless options through which to personalise their choices, and many media institutions are struggling to survive, radio has successfully continued to evolve. The increasing popularity of podcasts is only one example of the flexible, transportable and creative options for engaging with radio. Yet where media democratisation is most often attributed to the digital revolution, the adaptability and accessibility of radio technology has defined its history.

Outlining the challenges of understanding the 'moving target' of radio in the digital age, Andrew Dubber describes the continuing role it plays in furthering democratic principles through strengthening communities, representing a site of political activism, and providing a tool for development (2014, p.150). Able to reach and empower the most geographically remote and socially isolated spaces in society, radio has been described as the most important medium for social change (Gray-Felder 2001, p.14). Where computer technology remains inaccessible to the world's poor, radio continues to be a significant tool for social and economic development (Buckley 2000), bypassing the barriers of internet connectivity and low literacy levels. In developing countries, it has played a central role in building and facilitating democratic participation, from opposition to Latin American military dictatorships in the 1960s and 1970s to similar processes in Asia and Africa today, 'as people repudiate the last dictators, the new voices emerge from various media, and radio is usually at the forefront' (Gray-Felder 2001, p.14).

Radio has always been a site where power is contested. The early history of the medium was shaped by a cycle of grassroots experimentation and appropriation by government and commercial forces. Douglas shows the opposing themes which characterise the early history of radio broadcasting, simultaneously cultivating a sense of nationhood and a validation of subculture (2004, p.11). She describes a cyclical 20-year pattern of control and resistance through which 'rebellions and anarchy were ultimately tamed and co-opted on the air, only to reappear through different technologies, formats and subgroups of listeners' (Douglas 2004, p.17). At the centre of this is a 'technical insurgency' (Douglas 2004) which continues to define radio as it evolves.

Local, cheap and relatively easy to maintain, radio lends itself to grassroots, independent projects. Yet the fast pace of change and ever-increasing quantity and range of activity and formats complicates any attempt to categorise it effectively. As David Hendy argues, 'it changes too quickly to let us "see" it properly' (2000, p.5). Radio theorists highlight the futility of applying essentialist definitions, recognising that it is socially constructed in different ways in different places at different times (Dubber 2014). Instead, radio can only be understood in terms of its technological and cultural context at any given time (Tacchi 2000; Douglas 2004). This ubiquitous yet elusive nature contributes to the democratic credentials of radio. Within the contemporary global media context, radio remains driven by grassroots activity which ensures a level of independence. As Douglas shows, radio's ability to reinvent itself so frequently means that corporate control can never grasp it completely (2004).

The democratic function of mass media has been colonised by commercial media power, dramatically reducing the public sphere potential of broadcasting as a site for informed political debate. Tracking a shift from collectivist principles to individualist patterns of communication and association, Daniel C. Hallin positions contemporary mass media as central to the rise of neoliberalism (2008). Where media organisations were intimately connected to the lives and identities of social groups, they now operate as professionally run enterprises, targeting 'individual citizens as consumers within political markets' (Hallin 2008, p.47). As Mitzi Waltz (2005) argues, this shift is central to the contemporary growth and significance of alternative and activist media.

Mass media representations support and reinforce powerful and influential elites while marginalising other groups (Atton 2001). In contrast, a growing range of non-commercial, alternative and community media operate as a means of expression for disempowered, disadvantaged and misrepresented groups, with radio maintaining a prominent role in the process. This expression strengthens internal identity and manifests in the outside world, enabling social change, a function highlighted throughout the *Community Media Matters* report (Meadows et al 2007, p.11). Mapping the sector in Australia, the authors argue that community media 'citizens' are empowered through increased capacity to participate in democratic processes. Drawing on Nico Carpentier, Rico Lie and Jan Servaes' link between community media and civil society (2003, p.58), the report highlights the multiple and complex ways through which activity fosters citizen participation in public life. Community radio provides opportunities for people to engage in making, organising, influencing and listening to their own media. These instances of 'micro-participation' then contribute to a broader 'macro-participation' where individuals actively adopt civic attitudes and perform a pivotal role within a healthy democracy (Meadows et al 2007, p.14).

The issues around media and democratic participation are even more complex in relation to prisoners, a group 'categorised as facing 'civil death' or treated as 'partial' or 'conditional' citizens' (Anderson 2012, p.27). As Anderson argues, where the target audience is unentitled to vote and essentially stripped of citizen status, rights and freedoms, engagement with radio becomes a form of citizenship (2012, p.17). She relates the notion of prisoners as the 'civil dead' to the early history of prisons, where the convicted were routinely stripped of legal rights such as property ownership and the ability to inherit. Those who were not sentenced to death by execution instead faced a civil death 'to emulate the results a natural death would produce' (Damaska 1968, p.351). Prisons are based on the loss of rights that include the removal of both liberty and citizenship yet the ability to maintain community connections is central to successful reintegration and the reduction of reoffending behaviours. Therefore, where citizenship is removed, it becomes even more vital that prisoners have access to opportunities to 'enact their citizenship through alternative means' (Anderson 2012, p.58).

Anderson's use of a citizens' media theoretical framework is particularly useful for examining the effects of prisoner engagement with radio. Focusing on what the programming is 'doing' and what participation means to those involved, the approach recognises the multiplicity of ways through which citizenship is enacted (2012, p.17). Developed by Clemencia Rodriguez (2001), the concept of citizens' media expands the understanding of alternative media beyond the ability to counterbalance the domination of mass media corporations. Where discussion of alternative media is framed within rigid categories of power, it fails to acknowledge and understand the diversity of media experiences and effects (Rodriguez 2001). Instead, Rodriguez stresses the need to rethink issues of power and turns to radical democracy theory (Mouffe 1992; McClure 1992) to highlight the multiple ways in which power is experienced and exercised on various levels in different contexts.

Radical democracy redefines citizenship beyond legal rights to a status that is expressed and enacted through participation in everyday political practices. Participation in media production then becomes an act of citizenship in which power is produced through practices that reshape the identities of the self, of others and of environments (Rodriguez 2001, p.19). When applied to the exploration of prisoners' media, radio not only functions as a vital source of information and debate but represents a means through which prisoners proactively construct identities, becoming a form of citizenship (Anderson 2012).

Government through radio

National Prison Radio functions both as institutional and alternative media. The above discussion considers prison radio within contemporary debate on media and democracy, placing the alternative media principles of access, participation and independence at the heart of the NPR model. Equally, radio developed in partnership with state agencies for use within the prison apparatus connects to ideas around broadcasting and social control. The capacity to balance these dual and often conflicting functions is central to the success of prison radio. The PRA plays a crucial role in the process, acting as an independent intermediary to balance the aims of prisoner empowerment with the state function of prisoner management. The ability to negotiate these positions is informed by discussion of the governmental function of broadcasting.

Radio may well take second place to television in the mass media stakes today, yet the impact of radio in rebuilding post-war societies in the 1920s and 1930s cannot be underestimated. The early history of the organisation and regulation of radio is widely understood as a government technique for reconfiguring national identities both in Europe and the US. The political and cultural potential of the medium has been recognised and fought over since its inception. Emerging during the First World War, the development of radio moved from what Stuart Hood describes as an era of 'diffused experimentation' (1979, p.16) to tight control and supervision, with governments and industry moving quickly to harness and regulate radio to inform public values, opinions and tastes.

By 1923 the use of radio across Europe was largely institutionalised: 'the state had established a satisfactory system of control over the new public medium of broadcasting and had seen to it that the system was one that had no feed-back' (Hood 1979, p.18). These post-war developments were met with corresponding interest among practitioners and radical theorists including Bertolt Brecht, Walter Benjamin and Theodor Adorno. Their work shows an early belief in the active role of the listener for increasing civic engagement (Brecht 1979, p.27). Brecht considered radio as an opportunity for building a public sphere and for promoting the development of civil society, allowing direct contact with the people while bypassing the ideological apparatuses of the state (Hartley 2000, p.155). Rather than existing as a one-sided instrument of distribution, Brecht recognised radio as a means to actively engage citizens in public life, with the ability to become 'the most wonderful public communication system imaginable' (1979, p.25). This utopian vision may not have been fully realised, but prison radio is indicative of the inherently participatory nature of radio when used to effectively engage with audiences.

David Goodman offers some useful insights into the early 'civic ambition' of radio and identifies the contradictory positions which characterise its history, 'between entertainment and education, commercial and civic roles, passive and active listening, compliant and resistant audiences' (2011, p.xiv). In contrast to the development of public broadcasting across Europe, the corresponding organisation of radio in the US began as a primarily commercial venture. Yet Goodman highlights the degree of government influence and control involved through regulation which stressed the public service responsibilities of broadcasters. He describes US radio as constructed around a dual civic and commercial paradigm, functioning simultaneously as civic legitimation and commercial venture. He implies a balanced coexistence between the two influences, leading to more cultural, educational and civic programming than the commercial sector alone would have provided (Goodman 2011). Drawing on Adorno and Horkheimer's critique of mass media (1991), Goodman (2011) differentiates between the 'commercial paradigm' mode of individualised, passive, compliant, one-way reception of media messages and the 'civic paradigm' form of active listening, where citizens are actively engaged in a two-way communication process. Although the system was privately owned and operated, effective listener engagement was recognised as central to the civic function, as illustrated by a statement from the US Commissioner of Education at the time, 'regardless of who owns these lines of communication or what authority operates them at any given time, it is essential for the preservation of democracy that they be used to represent the American people and not to dictate to them' (Goodman 2011, p.69).

The growth of radio is inextricably linked to its construction as a 'social good'. Early broadcast regulation and organisation built on the transformative potential and therapeutic effects of radio. Whether in relation to healing the hospitalised (Taylor 2002); rehabilitating injured French war veterans (Scales 2008); or supporting the bedridden (Kirkpatrick 2011), listening was recognised as a form of civic and political engagement, a concept which was invoked to justify government control and commercial expansion from the outset. Bill Kirkpatrick provides an interesting and relevant example, identifying a proliferation of references to the 'shut-in' in the development of early US broadcasting policy. Describing those physically and socially isolated through long-term hospitalisation or homebound infirmity, radio was considered a 'blessed boon' through which to reconnect with society (Kirkpatrick 2011). In a similar pattern to that of Europe in the post-war period, the state became increasing concerned with the control and regulation of two-way amateur radio and the attempt to turn radio into 'a loudspeaker not a microphone' (2011, p.171).

Radio was quickly hailed as a social and cultural 'marvel', represented as 'the herald of civilisation bringing culture to the literal or figurative wilderness' (Kirkpatrick 2011, p.166), echoing the contemporary democratisation claims of new media. For Kirkpatrick, by invoking the shut-in as the perfect passive listener, state regulation of the airwaves was justified as a noble social good, and radio repositioned as playing a role in the management of society (2011, p.172). The co-articulation of disability and radio is presented as central to the process, shaping the social meanings of both, and operating as media policy, as disability policy, and as governmentality more generally. Kirkpatrick shows the ways in which the benefits of radio for people with disabilities were repeatedly used to support the case for the establishment of high-powered, commercially owned, national radio services. Broadcasting was defined in moral terms, and the audience imagined as passive recipients in need of 'quality' culture 'provided by trusted stewards of the airwaves' (2011, p.174).

There are obvious parallels with the experience of the 1920s shut-in and that of the prisoner, not only as confined to one location, but as excluded from civic participation. Where Kirkpatrick describes people with disabilities as regarded as socially 'in'-valid, partial citizens, cut off from any real participation in the community or economic life, prisoners are similarly stripped of citizenship. Kirkpatrick demonstrates the historical link between broadcasting and governance arguing that the discourses and procedures through which broadcasting and disability were connected provide insight into how media structures and policies come to regulate, conduct and redefine the parameters of citizenship (2011, p.168). Through focusing on the earliest inception of radio, he shows social exclusion as helping Americans to think about radio in particular ways at a historical moment when its purposes and structures were being defined. By 1930, the process was complete, with radio 'cleared to beam into every home the discourses of good citizenship and the proper and normal conduct of conduct' (2011, p.182).

However, where Kirkpatrick suggests that the social benefits of radio were identified and appropriated as a means of achieving the market interests of the 1920s modern liberal state, prison radio differs. The shut-in are presented as a passive audience whose unique, therapeutic relationship with radio was recognised and utilised to further the commercial aims of early US broadcasting policy. The distribution format of prison radio essentially remains one-way, yet through an emphasis on the role of prisoners as an active audience with the power to influence and create content, the PRA model bears a greater resemblance to the Brechtian ideal of two-way communication that facilitates participation in public life and civil society.

Defining public service broadcasting

The evolution of public service broadcasting (PSB) across Europe during the same period similarly builds on the socially transformative potential of broadcasting. The BBC remains the world's most famous cultural institution, widely considered as the model for PSB worldwide (Born 2004, p.95). Yet the story is one of contradictions, simultaneously considered as a form of cultural standardisation as well as being recognised as a crucial institution of civil society (Scannell 1989, p.136).

Analysis of the changing role of the BBC is central to the understanding of the development of the PRA, not only in terms of practical involvement, but in relation to the broader discussion of the democratic function of broadcasting. For discussion of the BBC's role in the founding years of the PRA in Chapter Four, I draw heavily on Georgina Born's (2004) definitive research on an institution in crisis as it strove to reinvent and defend itself against a tide of managerialism and marketisation. Her detailed analysis helps to contextualise prison radio activity, framing BBC interest as an attempt to demonstrate diversity and redefine a public 'service' function. Where the contemporary BBC context sets the scene for PRA growth, the institutional function of prison radio should also be considered in terms of the broader historical, cultural and political significance of broadcasting.

While often perceived as the one-way voice of the state, the BBC broadcast model was able to achieve Brecht's 'public service' function to a degree (Hartley 2000). As John Hartley shows, early radio came to symbolise civil society and community, becoming a site for the establishment of national identity through national culture (2000, p.156). Along with others (Hartley 2000; Crissell 2002; Hajkowski 2010), Scannell places PSB at the centre of forming national identity in post-war Britain. PSB played a significant role in democratising public life, creating the notion of a 'general' public through opening up of state occasions and public events for the first time, 'the fundamental democratic thrust of broadcasting lay in the new kind of access to virtually the whole spectrum of public life that radio first made available to all' (Scannell 1989, p.140).

Scannell argues that radio was responsible for creating a shared 'culture in common' for the first time. Through addressing the whole of society, PSB gradually came to represent the whole of society, giving 'a voice to the voiceless and faces to the faceless' (Scannell, 1989, p.142). The BBC's status as a 'public good' is justified through the universal distribution and availability of its services, producing a range of content that has become 'deeply known and taken for granted, bedded down in the very fabric of daily life for all of us' (Scannell 1989, p.138). Despite criticisms of the BBC serving the interests of the ruling class elite, broadcasting created new communicative entitlements to excluded social groups, shedding light on the social issues of unemployment, poverty and housing that had not previously been visible.

Broadcasting brought public life into private life, and vice versa, continually extending the range of what could be talked about in the public domain (Scannell 1989, p.144). However, even Scannell's vigorous defence of PSB recognises the delicate balance between public service and political and cultural control. He acknowledges that the whole history of the relationship between broadcasting and politics is one of manipulation and pressure through news content, political discussions and direct regulation, but critiques the tendency among academics to focus on the manipulative power of media, as a force able to beguile and indoctrinate unwitting audiences (Scannell, 1989, p.135). Instead, Scannell shows the interplay between state and public factors, arguing that PSB has been driven by both political and moral influences all along, with public opinion shaping state regulation. His argument is unequivocal, defending the status of the BBC as a public good that has 'unobtrusively contributed to the democratisation of everyday life, in public and private contexts, from its beginning through to this day' (Scannell, 1989, p.136).

In 1989, Scannell's defence of PSB came in response to attempts by Margaret Thatcher's government to deregulate public broadcasting. This process has continued to intensify since, with the social function of the BBC under mounting pressure from the concentration of commercial media power. Marking the start of media deregulation, Scannell argues that the 1984 Peacock Report represented the privatisation of information, culture and entertainment, redefining broadcasting as a commodity rather than a public good (1989, p.139). Instead of increasing and diversifying the range of media services, the commodification of PSB counteracts the principles of universal access to cultural resources, destabilising the fundamentally democratic principles on which it was based (Scannell 1989, p.139).

Born's view from inside the BBC during the 1990s focuses on this controversial period and outlines the organisational shifts which set the scene for involvement with prison radio. She describes globalisation and digitalisation as creating a critical juncture for national broadcasters by the early 2000s with the BBC struggling to reinvent itself in the face of rapid social, economic, political and technological changes (Born, 2002). While the BBC has historically enjoyed a unique position between commercial monopoly and government control, Born's work presents an institution suffering a crisis of identity and creativity in the aftermath of Thatcher's governments, New Labour interventionism, and the continuation of the neoliberal economic agenda. The period marks key changes and challenges which remodel the concept and function of public service and create the conditions of possibility for the development of independently run, socially focused prison radio provision.

The PRA is at once the product of the new opportunities for innovation presented through the neoliberal reworking of non-commercial media while remaining committed to the public service principles of accessibility, diversity and quality. As will be shown later, the PRA was established with the support of the BBC through an early partnership project. Yet equally, the growth of prison radio at the time is related to the dual pressures of commercialism and technological innovation that have destabilised the status of PSB. Digitalisation has increased the range and accessibility of media platforms, while deregulation has opened up the broadcast 'market', bringing the privileged position of the BBC as the sole distributor of universal cultural resources into question.

The development of prison radio indicates new models of non-commercial media practice that demonstrate the enduring relevance of PSB values in the context of rapid political, cultural and technological change. Scannell's defence of the BBC as essential to democratic functioning remains relevant today. Yet where national broadcasting across Europe and the US played a clear role in defining a 'general' public, bringing communities together to rebuild post-war nation states, the dual forces of globalisation and digitalisation have created multiple, diverse publics. The PRA is representative of new models of media practice working together with multiple and previously unrecognised publics. This both changes the nature of PSB and provides opportunities to extend its reach. Rather than a single broadcast institution addressing a single general public, PSB values are now dispersed through a proliferation of grassroots, countercultural media opportunities which continue to develop radio as a social good.

Summary

This chapter has examined the existing theories and literature around the origins and evolution of radio as a socially transformative medium. The growth of prison radio is connected to changes in the ways that both PSB and alternative media are organised, conceptualised and understood. Prison radio is uniquely positioned, based on non-mainstream, alternative media principles of empowerment, participation and representation while performing an institutional function, connected to the management of the prison population. The independent status of the PRA is central to the process, enabling prison radio to represent the rights of prisoners while working in partnership with state agencies. In these terms, the PRA operates as an intermediary between the state and civil society, between PSB and community radio, and between mainstream and alternative media, a role that will be further demonstrated in later chapters. Having placed PRA development within a wider broadcast context, the following chapter examines changing ideas around prisoners and punishment in order to understand a prison environment in which radio became utilised and encouraged.

2

'Making Waves Behind Bars': The Prison Context

To celebrate the official launch of the organisation as a charity in 2006, the first PRA audio productions to be distributed to an audience beyond the prisons were compiled on the *Making Waves Behind Bars* CD (PRA 2006). In the title, 'making waves' refers to radio broadcasting and audio editing technology, and equally indicates the potential for change and disruption 'behind bars'. The origins and potential of prison radio can only be examined through discussion of the complex and enduring problem of the prison institution. This chapter begins by outlining some of the key ideas that inform our understanding of the changing role and function of prison and punishment before examining the political, economic and institutional changes which have contributed to the recognition, acceptance and encouragement of radio in the prisons of England and Wales.

Worldwide, the function of prison has become a critical issue, characterised by a rapid increase of incarceration rates, a failure to effectively reduce reoffending, and the exponential criminalisation of marginalised groups. Women are the fastest growing prison population (Davis 2003, p.65) and the dramatic overrepresentation of people of colour and of First Nations Peoples in prisons across the US, Europe, South America, Australia and New Zealand highlight vast inequalities of justice. There are over 11 million people behind bars worldwide (Walmsley 2016). The rate of growth of global prison populations is staggering, increasing over five times in just three decades (Wacquant 2003). In the late 2000s alone, prison numbers grew in 78% of all countries (Dreisinger 2017). Of these, the US represents the highest incarceration rates of any country by far, imprisoning around 1% of the adult population at any time (Harcourt 2010). In England and Wales prison numbers doubled in two decades (Ministry of Justice 2013) and the likelihood of returning to prison is recorded as high as 59% for those serving sentences of less than 12 months (Open Justice 2017).

Over the past half century, prison theorists recognise a fundamental shift in the ways that crime and punishment are conceptualised (Feeley and Simon 1992; Garland 1997; Wacquant 2009; Sim 2009). Whether the dramatic rise of the prison population is considered as a symptom of wider socio-economic breakdown (Sim 2009) or as central to the functioning and expansion of the neoliberal state (Wacquant 2009), all highlight the impact of combining neoliberal rationalities and practices with the 'business' of punishment. The role of the prison has been dramatically reconfigured, shaped by multiple and often conflicting themes including privatisation, the contracting out of service provision, managerialism, and a punitive shift in attitudes to crime driven by populist political rhetoric. It is a contradictory context which has led to an institutional crisis that extends beyond practical issues of funding and overcrowding, underpinned by a crisis of identity and legitimacy connected to the moral and ethical implications of the economic reworking of punishment.

Unlike in the US, only 15% of prisons in England and Wales are managed by private companies. Due to the combined factors of worsening overcrowding and underperformance against government contract targets, the privatisation project appears to be slowing (Bastow 2013), yet the contract value remains over £4 billion per year. In what has become an abolitionist manifesto, Angela Davis (2003) describes the increasing and worrying alliance between government and corporate worlds in the business of prisons. The cash profits are relatively low compared to other corporate interests, but the prison industrial complex is playing an increasingly central role in the economic functioning of many advanced western democracies. It is an industry which encompasses the broader penal system of police, surveillance, probation, courts, legal services, and immigration detention, representing an increasingly embedded and dispersed network with a vested interest in maintaining a steady flow of criminalised and displaced people. The reach expands beyond the construction and management of buildings to the provision of goods and services within the estate, from meals to hygiene goods, healthcare and therapy. Companies that would not necessarily be involved in state punishment have developed major stakes in the perpetuation of a prison system whose obsolescence then becomes more difficult to achieve (Davis 2003, p.88).

Punishment is a complex social, ideological and cultural terrain that will never be an entirely rational execution of orders with clear objectives and controllable outcomes. As Jane Andrew argues, it has 'multiple and competing aims and innumerable intended and unintended consequences' (2007, p.898). The neoliberal prison normalises the connection between punishment and profit, yet the notion of punishing people for profit links profit to pain and suffering, a situation which Mick Ryan and Tony Ward describe as 'morally repugnant' (1989, p.70). Punishment in itself is not the issue; instead, it is the socio-political message that private ownership sends through the 'rewards that accrue to penal entrepreneurs' (Ryan and Ward 1989, p.70). The possibility for profit creates a vested interest in prison expansion and the risk that prisoners will suffer abuse and exploitation for profit (Andrew 2007).

The contemporary prison debate is defined by a punitive turn in political policy and rhetoric together with the privatisation and corporatisation of government services. Through neoliberal governmental rationalities and technologies, the function of prison has moved from rehabilitation to management. National

Prison Radio represents resistance against individualised approaches to crime control, providing a communitarian response to the causes of incarceration and recidivism, placing those with lived prison experience at the centre of discussion on potential ways to reduce imprisonment. In a context of institutional crisis, prison radio offers an innovative, enterprising and relatively low-cost means of managing the prison population and supporting the entrepreneurial prisoner to 'invest' in their future through education and information. Equally, PRA discourse and practice demonstrates a commitment to prisoner rights, rehumanising the neoliberal position and performing a crucial role in bringing issues of social justice and social welfare back into the equation.

Prison and power

The humanity with which a government treats its prisoners is regarded as a benchmark of its democratic principles and values (Lacey 2008). In 1831, Alexis de Tocqueville toured American prisons with Gustave de Beaumont as part of a study of the nation's democracy. While extolling the virtues of free commerce, industry and capitalism, he decried the effects of social isolation and anxiety imposed on the prisoners, 'the United States gives the example of the most extended liberty, the prisons of that same country offer the spectacle of the most complete despotism' (de Beaumont and de Tocqueville 1833, p.47). These observations remain strikingly relevant today. As Loïc Wacquant argues, the contemporary resurgence of incarceration not only marks the continuation of such despotic control but extends its reach beyond the prison walls to the neoliberal regulation of social marginality (2009, p.314).

The rapid expansion of the prison estate is connected to major economic and political shifts of the 1970s and 1980s, linked to economic deregulation, the dismantling of welfarism, and the individualisation of responsibility, the same themes which have transformed the organisation of media and social activism discussed elsewhere in this study. However, the inevitable and undisputed status of the prison institution makes any attempt to address its dysfunctions difficult to achieve. Prison has become normalised as a response to crime even though imprisonment only began to emerge as the dominant form of punishment in the mid-18th century. Those suspected of committing a crime were locked up prior to this, but as a means of awaiting sentence, whether hanging, flogging, fine or banishment (Klare 1973). Through a relatively short history, prison has developed an iconic status and a deeply embedded ideological presence (Sim 2009, p.16), continuing to be the most controversial of institutions, generating deep-seated disputes and ongoing political debate (Carrabine et al 2004, p.289).

Prison is not only a place where society locks away those it deems to be criminal, it performs a deeper, symbolic enactment of power. Michel Foucault's *Discipline and Punish: the Birth of the Prison* (1991, originally published in 1975) remains the central reference point for the study of power and punishment. His investigation into the emergence of the prison is used as a means of exploring the much wider theme of how domination is achieved, and how individuals are socially constructed in the world. Foucault examines ways in which disciplinary regimes exercise power, presenting discipline as a form of self-regulation encouraged by institutions and permeating modern societies (Mills 2003, p.43). The prison becomes symbolic of changing forms of power, from sovereignty where power is dispersed from above, to disciplinary, where power is exercised through the social body.

The study begins with the graphic account of a 1757 execution in Paris in which the accused is paraded through the streets in a public spectacle designed to have maximum effect on the audience as much as the victim. Through a lengthy and gruesome process, the flesh is torn from his body and combinations of molten lead, boiling oil, burning resin, wax and sulphur poured on his wounds before he is drawn and quartered and finally consumed by fire (Foucault 1991, p.3). The depiction serves to illustrate the brutal enactment of sovereign power and provides a stark contrast to the reformative aims of the early prison institution. Based on the moral rehabilitation of the criminal through prayer, contemplation and penitence, the birth of the prison represents the turning point from punishment of the body to discipline of the soul.

Foucault's discussion of the panopticon illustrates the process through which disciplinary power is exercised, not only within the prison but representative of wider institutional techniques of surveillance which monitor behaviours and instil self-governance. Designed by philosopher and reformer, Jeremy Bentham (2008 [1791]), the architectural panopticon or 'inspection house', is based on a circular structure built around a central inspection tower, allowing for constant and individualised surveillance of isolation cells designed for prayer and contemplation. It symbolises the automatic functioning of disciplinary power, described as 'the diagram of the mechanism of power reduced to its ideal form' (Foucault 1991, p.205) through inducing a state of conscious and permanent visibility. The panoptic gaze is an embedded and increasingly dispersed governmental technique, yet disciplinary practice has shifted away from concern with the moral reform of individuals towards risk management of social groups.

First published in 1975, Foucault's work came on the cusp of major political and economic shifts which triggered the exponential growth of the prison complex. David Garland's description of the emergence of a *Culture of Control* (2001) builds on Foucault's work, representing the next pivotal shift in the analysis of crime and social order. The social, economic and cultural forces of late modernity have redefined the meanings and policy around crime and punishment, shifting from issues of welfare to problems of control. Garland highlights the decline of the rehabilitative model of prisons and the rise of actuarial techniques of risk management in relation to punishment. His writings throughout the 1990s show a growing sense of doubt and dissatisfaction around modern penal practices stemming from rising crime rates and prison unrest at the end of the 1960s, 'it has become one of the most perplexing and perpetual crisis [sic] of modern social life' (Garland 1990, p.4).

However, the failure of the prison is central to its enduring success as a means of wider political domination. The negative impact of prisons has been recognised and criticised from as early as the 1820s, including the failure to reduce crime, tendency to increase recidivism, and the pressure inflicted on prisoners' families (Garland 1990, p.149). As Foucault (1991) argues, prison has always been a penological failure, yet its continued survival lies in its political effects on a wider social level.

The problems of crime and punishment have been progressively politicised over the past 50 years, with prison increasingly utilised as a primary technology of social regulation. The economic crisis and social insecurities of the 1960s and 1970s led to the political ascension of neoliberal authoritarianism. World leaders such as Margaret Thatcher and Ronald Reagan were instrumental in reframing the collective experience and political meaning of crime and welfare throughout the 1980s (Garland and Sparks 2000, p.199). A reactionary mix of free-market economics, anti-welfare social policy and cultural conservatism produced an unprecedented acceleration of imprisonment. Stuart Hall and colleagues (2013 [1978]) offer the most vivid account of this period. Through the analysis of the social construction of 'mugging' in 1970s Britain, they demonstrate the ways in which street crime was raised in the public consciousness and used to legitimate more coercive methods of social control amid social, economic and racial unrest.

Similarly, Garland's analysis of 'delinquency' highlights the symbolic function of incarceration (1990). The creation of a delinquent class has advantages that perform a key role in a strategy of political domination: 'it works to separate crime from politics, to divide the working classes against themselves, to enhance the fear of prison, and to guarantee the authority and powers of the police' (Garland 1990, p.150). As individualised, small attacks on property or authority, delinquency primarily affects victims from lower classes, presenting little political danger. Such criminality is tolerated by the authorities, within certain limits, ensuring that repeat offenders are known by the authorities and contributing to improved management and surveillance. On a wider level, the predatory nature of delinquency makes it unpopular with other members of the working class and the myths of dangerousness that develop add to the process of distancing and division. Therefore, the prison does not control the criminal so much as control the working class by creating the criminal. For Foucault, this is the unspoken rationale for the persistence of the prison institution, where the unintended consequences of imprisonment that were first seen as detrimental are subsequently recognised, reinforced and deliberately employed (Garland 1990, p.150).

Garland's work is essential for understanding the shift in crime control away from traditional social and legal frameworks towards neoliberal managerial techniques; from collective welfarist responses to problems of individual responsibility. Prison is used to normalise and reinforce dominant values and regiment individuals, protecting society from the 'irresponsible behaviours of a dangerous and undeserving underclass' (Garland and Sparks 2000, p.200), those who abuse the freedoms of capitalism and make life impossible for the rest of us. For Garland, high crime rates and rising prison numbers represent a fundamental political failing. Yet where he describes a gradual and evolutionary response to the socio-economic insecurities of late modernity, Wacquant presents an abrupt and revolutionary process in which the rise of the prison state is an explicit political project, central to the advancement of neoliberalism.

For Wacquant, the rise of the prison state marks a major political transformation of the last half century (2009, p.xiii), 'becoming increasingly active and intrusive in the lower regions of social space' (2003, p.11). He offers a dramatic and expansive critique of the prison as central to the neoliberal governance of the poor, indicating an increased reliance on the police and penal institutions to control the disorders produced by mass unemployment, wage insecurity and diminishing social protection (Wacquant 2003, p.13). Where liberalism is evident in terms of markets, the state is increasingly punitive towards the poor, illustrating a central paradox of neoliberalism, that those who called for the end of 'big government' are the same as those who currently glorify the penal state (Wacquant 2003). Rather than being contradictory themes, Wacquant sees both as being essential components of a new institutional machinery for managing poverty. Where imprisonment functions as a protection against the fallout of global capitalism, it simultaneously reinforces and strengthens neoliberal ideology by demonising those who fail to 'succeed' in terms of free-market values.

In a society that values enterprise and profit, those who fail to reinforce those values present a risk by undermining the belief that everyone has equal opportunity to flourish. Arguing that the current revival of the prison institution is central to a 'government of social insecurity', Wacquant shows the invisible hand of the market as combining with the iron fist of the state to make the lower classes accept a deregulated labour market and the social issues that it creates (2003, p.14). Prisons therefore disguise the socio-economic impact of global capitalism on people by imprisoning the products of political and economic alienation (Andrew 2007, p.883).

Crisis and opportunity

Wacquant's analysis of mass incarceration strategies in the US (2009) highlights the global expansion of neoliberal penality and offers useful insights for understanding developments in the UK.

Yet, as Nicola Lacey (2010) argues, it is important to differentiate between global jurisdictions in order to identify opportunities for resistance. Populist, punitive political responses to crime and punishment may be an inevitable feature of contemporary democracies, yet key institutional differences between national systems remain intact (Lacey 2010, p.781). Having examined the broader themes that define the contemporary prison debate, attention now turns to the unique cultural, political and institutional conditions which have contributed to the emergence of UK prison radio. As Lacey states, 'only by understanding the institutional preconditions for a tolerant criminal justice system can we think clearly about the possible options for reform within particular systems' (2010, p.781).

National Prison Radio emerged from a context of radical change shaped by a punitive political turn in attitudes to crime, and the associated operational crisis of a prison system struggling to manage a dramatic rise in prisoner numbers within outdated and inadequate facilities. Paul McDowell, PRA Trustee and former HM Chief Inspector of Probation, has been connected to prison radio since the early days of Radio Feltham. During his time as governor of HMP Brixton, he played a central role in the development of Electric Radio Brixton and, subsequently, NPR. Reflecting on the beginnings of the project, he highlights the challenges of the prison at the time, describing overcrowding and a severe shortage of space, facilities and activities (McDowell 2012). With a population of around 900 inmates at any time, opportunities for prisoner activities were limited to only half of the people for half of the prison day, a total of three hours. In a 'negative and depressing' environment, where staff were 'surviving' from day to day, and prisoners had nothing to do, radio was recognised as a practical solution, making use of limited space to generate as wide an impact as possible, "something interesting that everyone could feel a part of" (McDowell 2012).

This picture is one which reflects a state of ever-deepening crisis across the prison system in England and Wales. Prison

Service support for the work of the PRA indicates a desire to identify effective, innovative, low-cost solutions to the range of challenges faced. However, where the term 'crisis' implies a short-lived critical point in time, the current status represents an enduring feature of recent decades which not only compromises the ability of the state to maintain order but challenges the moral sensibilities around the purpose of prisons (Carrabine et al 2004, p.289). The practical challenges of managing a rapidly increasing prison population are widely recognised. Yet the situation extends beyond practical and material issues, exacerbated by a crisis of legitimacy and connected to one of self-definition (Carrabine et al 2004, p.290).

Prison overcrowding has become normalised in a state of 'chronic capacity stress' (Bastow 2013). In contrast to the solitary and serene contemplation of Bentham's vision, multiple men are now occupying cells originally designed for one prisoner. The HM Chief Inspector of Prisons for England and Wales (2017) describes the appalling conditions in which many prisoners are held, locked up for close to 23 hours per day and eating meals in a shared cell next to an unscreened toilet. This is coupled with accounts of insect and vermin infestations and 'filthy and dilapidated' shower and toilet facilities without plans for refurbishment. A constant status of severe staff shortages, insufficient training and inadequate facilities lead to staff demoralisation and prisoner frustration, contributing to the rapid deterioration of safety in prisons.

In 2017, violence in prisons reached record numbers, with 26,643 assaults recorded within 12 months, including attacks on staff equating to an average of 20 a day (Ministry of Justice 2017a). The Ministry of Justice Safety in Custody statistics show record increases in assaults and incidents of self-harm, rising more than 70 percent from 2013 to 2016 (Ministry of Justice 2017a). During the same period, the number of self-inflicted deaths in custody has more than doubled, with 113 people ending their own lives in the 12 months to March 2017

(HM Inspectorate of Prisons 2017, p.7). Women entering prison are revealed as a particularly vulnerable group through a dramatic rise in incidence of self-harm and the self-inflicted deaths of 12 women within 12 months, events which are even more significant given the slight overall reduction in the female prison population during the same period (HM Inspectorate of Prisons 2017).

The many and complex reasons for a dramatic decline in safety in prisons is connected to chronically low staffing levels which limit the ability to let prisoners out of their cells to have access to facilities, exercise, training and education. The HM Inspectorate of Prisons 2017 *Annual Report* highlights time in cells as a major factor in the decline of safety:

> Our expectation is that prisoners should be unlocked for at least 10 hours a day. According to our prisoner survey, only 14 percent of prisoners achieve this, and the figure is as low as four percent for young adults and eight percent in local prisons. Shockingly, 30 percent of young adults (aged 18 to 21) being held in adult establishments told us that they spent less than two hours a day out of their cells. (HM Inspectorate of Prisons 2017, p.9)

Again, current issues can be traced back to the 1970s, with a dramatic rise in UK prison numbers connected to the deepening economic crisis of the time (Sim 2009, p.28), and its effects on what Steven Box describes as the criminalisation of subordinate groups:

> Prisons are being used to punish more and more offenders and particularly the young. They are also being used to serve as a warning to those not deserving imprisonment this time round. (Box, 1983, p.207)

The subject of prisons was raised in the public consciousness through a series of bitter industrial disputes between prison staff and managers, and concerns about severe overcrowding and conditions so bad that even prison governors spoke out in the press (Sim 2009). The governor of HMP Wormwood Scrubs described himself as "the manager of a large penal dustbin" while the governor of Strangeways (now HMP Manchester) described conditions in the prison as "an affront to civilised society" (Sim 2009, p.30).

Joe Sim argues that these factors combined to undermine the legitimacy of the institution, symbolising a broader hegemonic crisis in the wider society (2009, p.26). Where the prisons of the state were no longer seen as contributing to the social order, Thatcher's Conservative Party was able to achieve a landslide election victory in 1979 through a government programme of law and order based on the principles of the free market and the strong state (Sim 2009, p.26). Stuart Hall responded at the time, 'Make no mistake about it: under this regime, the market is to be Free; the People are to be Disciplined' (1980, p.5). This status reflected the drive towards the social authoritarianism of Thatcher's first government, indicating the intensification of state power (Sim 2009, p.28), a position which has since been adapted and strengthened by successive governments on both sides of the political spectrum. By 1993, the prisoner population in England and Wales reached record levels of 41,800. In just two decades, the number almost doubled, reaching 86,000 by 2012 (Ministry of Justice 2013).

The distinctive New Labour brand of populist punitivism provides the backdrop for the growth of UK prison radio in the late 1990s and early 2000s. As Wacquant (2009) argues, neoliberalism is not only a project of the right. The New Labour governments oversaw the biggest prison expansion in the country's history, with the prison population rising by 40% between 1997 and 2010 (Garrett 2014, p.94). The law and order debate was central to the reinvention of the Labour Party with

Tony Blair, as Shadow Home Secretary, successfully wrestling the issue away from the government. While in opposition, New Labour rose to power on the back of a 'tough on crime' policy agenda and continued to establish their role in the minds of the public as the party who would instigate tough and effective measures against those who broke the law.

As Ian Brownlee (1998) demonstrates, the New Labour approach was inherently contradictory, combining punitive political rhetoric with a focus on social justice. The progressive components of the regime included an increase in community sentencing and a commitment to reducing reoffending, yet policy remained predominantly based on a 'criminology of the other' (Brownlee 1998, p.316), with political rhetoric instilling fear of crime into the public and emphasising individual factors including 'fecklessness and wickedness'. Referring to the rise of the 'New Penology' (Feeley and Simon 1992), Brownlee outlines a move away from humanitarian ideals and values towards a bureaucratised, efficiency-driven model. Within this context, criminal justice policy and practice performs a managerial rather than an aspirational or transformative function, and relates to the wider policy environment of public sector managerialism based on a common discourse of new techniques for organising and governing social life (Brownlee, 1998, p.323).

The New Penology theory was developed at the height of Conservative Party punitive penal policy and rhetoric. Feeley and Simon (1992) critique the prison function, arguing that it is no longer based on either punishment or rehabilitation, but on management through variable detention based on risk assessment. The observations were made only five years before New Labour came to power in the UK. Rather than restoring the principles of rehabilitation and reintegration, New Labour succeeded in extending the managerial reach of the New Penology through the appropriation of a discourse of education, empowerment and transformation. Penal policy and practice has been restructured through a focus on targets and

Key Performance Indicators for reducing reoffending (Home Office 2004) which further serve to categorise and manage unruly groups according to differentiated risk factors rather than 'aspirations to rehabilitate, reintegrate and retrain' (Feeley and Simon 1992, p.457).

Feeley and Simon (1992) acknowledge the increase in projects and programmes that were beginning to emerge within the prison system at the time. Where they concede that the long-term effects were yet to be seen, they remained cynical about the possibilities for change (1992, p.463). Despite the 'lingering language' of rehabilitation and reintegration, innovative projects are presented in terms of managing costs and controlling dangerous populations rather than focusing on social and personal transformation (1992, p.452). However, over 25 years later, prison radio growth demonstrates a further reworking of rehabilitation that combines a managerial function with a focus on prisoner empowerment. The PRA works collaboratively with voluntary and statutory sector agencies to connect prisoners to a range of information and services. Rather than initiatives 'imposed' on unwilling subjects to achieve managerial outputs, outside organisations and agencies are increasingly involved in working together with prisoners and prison staff to provide services. Considered as a reaction to the negative institutional and personal impact of the New Penology, prison radio bridges the managerial needs of the prison with the individual needs of the prisoner.

The growth of prison radio is both a product of, and a reaction against, the extension of market rationalities and managerial processes throughout the penal system, functioning through devolved responsibility and partnerships between state, public, private and non-profit sectors. Access to information and support is promoted through daily NPR programming as well as through regular social action campaigns, with examples ranging from a series of short promotional features on drug and alcohol awareness, to a one-day focus on smoking, and a month-long campaign about learning to read while in prison. In response to an identified increased risk of self-inflicted deaths and self-harm throughout the month of January, a 2017 series encouraged prisoners to talk about how they are feeling, particularly if they are struggling to cope with life inside. It features interviews and first night testimonies designed to break the taboo surrounding depression, informing prisoners of the signs that someone may be at risk and giving clear information about some of the processes and policies they may come into contact with in prison (PRA 2017a). Such programming represents a coordinated and collaborative approach to ensuring that prisoners have access to rehabilitation and resettlement support.

The continued independent status of the PRA prioritises the voice and expression of prisoners, remaining focused on the representation of prison issues in their own terms. This view is supported by Tom Allan (2006) through his observation of *Radio Wanno* at HMP Wandsworth, arguing that the major achievement of prison radio is the ability to invert the philosophy of the panopticon. Rather than the isolated, faceless deviant as a subject of constant surveillance, prison radio production activity encourages and empowers prisoners to engage and participate.

Referring to the ongoing prison reform debate, Allan highlights the controversy of empowering prisoners and giving them opportunities (2006, p.22). The primary function of prisons is incapacitation, to punish the prisoner and protect the public from potential harm; yet focusing on incapacitation alone is as harmful to society as it is to the individual. Locking people away may remove the threat but also removes responsibility for family, work or home, and therefore the capacity to make responsible decisions on release. Where the isolation of the panopticon severs relationships and community links vital for successful rehabilitation, prison radio initiatives seek to build human relationships between prisoners, families and prison staff (Allan 2006, p.22).

Allan illustrates the process through the example of prison radio work with the *Family Man* courses run by non-profit group *Safe Ground* since 2003, using drama and creativity to support prisoners to develop and maintain family relationships. This extends to the *Story Book Dads* and *Story Book Mums* projects, which have worked closely with multiple prison radio stations to enable mothers and fathers in prison to record bedtime stories for their children to listen to. For Allan (2006, p.22), this is indicative of the ways in which human relationships, rather than isolation, are being recognised as the solution.

Radio is representative of the increased range of rehabilitation programmes and activities available in prison, with NPR providing information on education and support to help prisoners to prepare for release. Yet despite such interventions, the challenges of life on the outside remain, with former prisoners facing social stigmatisation and significant financial and accommodation problems. While rehabilitation initiatives seek to strengthen relationships, the role of prison in society remains one of separation, illustrating the continued tension between 'the history of authoritarian control and dehumanisation, and a modernity that sometimes demands, with moral and legal force, that prisoners' rights be protected' (Allan 2006, p.23).

As the PRA story demonstrates, the reality of the prison role and function lies between the two influences. Prison remains an institution for punishment, satisfying an ancient public need for visible retribution as well as supporting the dominant social order by disciplining disaffected social groups, while simultaneously adopting the 'modern mission' to reintegrate and remake prisoners as law abiding citizens. It is a difficult balance to achieve where education opportunities and therapeutic interventions available inside fail to translate to the practicalities of gaining employment and housing outside. Allan describes it as a 'schizophrenic position', where we are unwilling to fully accept former prisoners back into society, yet unwilling to reject them completely (2006, p.23). Despite a discourse of rehabilitation playing a prominent role in penal policy and practice, prison still serves a decisive social function of separation, defined through disciplinary mechanisms based on the binary branding of normal and abnormal, legal and illegal or safe and unsafe (Foucault 1991, p.199). It is a role that is deeply embedded, providing a means of isolating and separating the deviant 'other' which 'comfortingly denies our own imperfections, depositing the dark side of human behaviour in the few' (Allan 2006, p.23).

NPR broadcasts behind the prison walls, yet the very existence of a radio service challenges outside assumptions about prisons and prisoners. Rather than a homogenous group of 'bad' people, prison radio highlights the fact that prisoners are individuals with a multitude of stories, backgrounds and experiences which have contributed to incarceration. This challenges the principles of separation, facilitating a discourse between those inside and outside of the criminal justice system, and revealing prisoners as complex individuals rather than 'the isolated silhouettes of the panopticon' (Allan 2006, p.23).

Summary

Punishment is inextricably connected to power, with prison performing both symbolic and material functions (Wacquant 2003, p.xv). This chapter began by establishing the status of prison as a representation of the wider function of disciplinary power in society before introducing the neoliberal rationalities and technologies which characterise the modern penal system. The UK backdrop from which the PRA emerged saw public services and institutions gradually restructured and privatised to varying degrees, with even the traditional state apparatus of the prison reinvented as a site of enterprise. The PRA is representative of increased numbers of non-profit organisations, education providers and social care agencies operating within an opened up, marketised prison sector. In the wake of institutional crisis and state withdrawal from welfare issues, such organisations play a vital role in balancing institutional managerial aims with a focus on the transformative potential of individual prisoners, a role I examine in the following chapter.

Working on a number of levels at a particular time, prison radio addresses the social issue of prisoner rights while also fitting with neoliberal responses to crime and punishment, representing innovation within the new 'enterprising' public sector, maximising impact for minimum spend. In these terms, prison radio is both a practical response to an institutional crisis and a resistance against the punitive rhetoric that drives penal policy. The PRA resists the economic reworking of punishment through an emphasis on prisoner agency, choice and opportunity, functioning as an intermediary between prisoner, institution and state. After outlining the changes in both the broadcasting and prison sectors from which the PRA emerged, the following chapter identifies comparable shifts in the non-profit sector, focusing on the people who founded and developed prison radio.

3

'Making a Difference': Social Action and Enterprise

As with any new social venture, the PRA story is driven by the people who instigated and developed the activity. When asked to reflect on what drew them to the idea of prison radio, PRA participants all talk of the potential to change the lives of prisoners, and of a continued commitment to 'making a difference'. This chapter focuses on the motivations, characteristics and actions of those involved in the process. I present prison radio growth as a product of a wider political and cultural context that has redefined volunteerism, social activism, and cultural production in terms of enterprise and entrepreneurship, in order to support the restoration of social welfare and growth of the knowledge-based economy. The contemporary political context placed innovation and enterprise at the centre of economic and social reform, qualities which PRA founders typified, developing a new, non-profit, creative service within the public sector. However, through discussion of literature on the reconfiguration of the non-profit sector and theories of social and creative entrepreneurship, I argue that the focus on economic functioning fails to adequately acknowledge the social values and motivations at the heart of the activity.

I begin by outlining the conditions and effects of the formalisation of the non-profit sector before discussing the unique political context of UK prison radio development. I then identify common characteristics of the people involved, dividing them into two overlapping groups: the volunteer founders and the original staff team. The aims and motivations behind the beginnings of prison radio are discussed in terms of volunteerism and social activism. Those that drove the establishment of the PRA and National Prison Radio are related to theories of social and creative entrepreneurship which increasingly inform voluntary and public sector practice. Interviews with those involved illustrate the continuation, crystallisation and evolution of PRA aims and objectives, based on core common values. The success of prison radio is achieved through an ongoing focus on accountability to the prisoner audience, collaborative working with non-profit and prison partners, and organisational independence to flexibly navigate an increasingly pressured and divisive non-profit environment.

In the preceding chapters, prison radio was discussed as both alternative and public service media, and as both a product of, and resistance against, neoliberal disciplinary practice. Here, activity is considered within the context of new arrangements for the contracting out of public services, epitomising a governmental shift towards a more enterprising, innovative and independent public sector. PRA discourse and practice remains focused on changing the lives of prisoners, representing resistance against the economic reworking of volunteerism, social activism and cultural production. The accounts of founders all highlight the importance of people over business targets and measures, demonstrating the enduring character of social activism in the context of managerialism and corporatisation.

The PRA is representative of an increased number of voluntary sector and civil society organisations involved in the provision of welfare and support services. Developing throughout the 2000s, and formally established in 2006, the PRA and its founders were able to navigate and negotiate a rapidly changing policy and funding environment in order to build a prisoner-led radio service. Through the examination of specific projects in later chapters, I explore the range of opportunities and challenges faced. Each of the examples, including the delivery of a prison radio education partnership project, demonstrates the reconfiguration of public services and ideas of social justice, and the role of the third sector in the process. Here, I outline existing theories on social activism, volunteerism and the non-profit sector which inform the later discussion of the people, partnerships and institutional arrangements through which prison radio was developed.

The non-profit sector

From the beginnings of Radio Feltham in the late 1990s to the current National Prison Radio partnership, the growth of the PRA can be tracked against the wider political and economic repositioning of the 'third sector', where organisations and agencies driven by social rather than profit motives have gained a new prominence in civic revival. As such, the actions of those involved in establishing the PRA, and subsequent organisational development, need to be considered within the wider context of the recognition, legitimation and professionalisation of the non-profit sector.

The PRA grew out of a policy context which recognised the social and economic potential of non-profit organisations working in partnership with state and private sectors to achieve social outcomes. However, the formalisation and professionalisation of the non-profit sector raises questions around the degree to which it conflicts with the aims of individual actors, dilutes social impact, and stifles the creativity and flexibility that define it. The PRA story reflects and represents the development of the sector itself, from informal, spontaneous activity to institutionalised service provision. The professionalisation, trust and state reliance on the voluntary sector has increased to the extent of supporting the development of creative projects in prisons, while the accounts of PRA founders illustrate both the possibilities and challenges of navigating and negotiating a rapidly shifting cultural and political landscape in order to achieve their original aims.

The Incite! anthology, *The Revolution Will Not be Funded* (2017), provides valuable observations on the emergence and effects of the non-profit industrial complex. While focused on developments in the US, the collective writings demonstrate the impact of global capitalism on changing forms of social welfare and social action. As with its military and prison antecedents, the critique refers to the impact of introducing the profit motive into the 'business' of providing social care and instigating social change. Prison radio links to shifts in social welfare provision, increasing access to specialist support services. When led by people with lived prison experience, it simultaneously represents social action, giving a voice to an unheard, socially excluded group and facilitating conversations about the realities of crime and crime control.

The non-profit sector encompasses a vast array of activity from large national and international organisations to grassroots and community based groups, all with different interests, ideologies and focus, and with varying capacity, infrastructure, and access to resources. Collectively, they represent a major contribution to national economies. In 2000, US non-profits controlled over $1.59 trillion in financial assets with expenditure of over $822 billion dollars (National Council of Non-profit Associations 2000). The combined income of all UK voluntary organisations was estimated at £39 billion in 2014, almost £10 billion more than the national university sector (Saxton and Kanemura 2015).

Again, contemporary shifts connect to the Thatcher/ Reagan era, and the combined social and economic fallout of deindustrialisation, financial deregulation and social welfare destruction. As governments absolve themselves of responsibility for the wellbeing of populations, the non-profit industry has grown to assume the role of providing essential services. As shown in previous chapters, state withdrawal paradoxically involves increased intervention to protect corporate and elite interests. The privatisation of social welfare is more insidious than a straightforward exchange of monies. Instead, an increasingly competitive environment is created through the major withdrawal of public funding, leading to the aggressive introduction of corporate rationalities and business models into the sector. As Munshi and Willse (2017, p.xvi) observe, this marks the greatest neoliberal achievement. Highlighting the cumulative effects of decades of neoliberal reform on exacerbating class, racial and gendered inequalities, they question the possibilities for transformative politics in the light of the neoliberal capacity for incorporating and neutralising demands for social justice (2017, p.xiv).

The 'Is Prison Obsolete?' conference is organised by *Sisters Inside*, an Australian community organisation working alongside women in prison to advocate for their human rights and address the gaps in services available to them. At the 2016 conference in Brisbane, representatives from international grassroots activist groups providing vital frontline services for and by criminalised women expressed increasing frustrations caused by the need to continually compete for funding with large, national and often faith-based organisations. These increasingly powerful, so called 'care bear' corporations win the largest share of government and philanthropic funding, and play a major role in the provision of social welfare services, which are often developed without meaningful consultation with their core service-user stakeholders.

As Paul Kivel (2017) argues, social services work needs to be combined with work for social change for any lasting impact. Where the continuation of the non-profit industrial complex is dependent on vast and continual numbers of people in need, many organisations have a vested interest in maintaining the status quo. Kivel outlines an important distinction: where social service work addresses the needs of individuals affected by the impact of institutional systems of exploitation and violence, social change work challenges the root cause of the exploitation and violence. Referring to the challenges faced by domestic and family violence prevention programmes, he argues that no matter how hard they work to support victims and educate perpetrators, there is limited impact on the systems that perpetuate violence:

> We also need to work for social change so that we create a society in which our institutions and organisations are equitable and just, and a society in which all people are safe, adequately fed and sheltered, well educated, afforded safe and decent jobs, and empowered to participate in the decisions that affect their lives. (Kivel 2017, p.130)

The industrial complex model provides a framework for understanding the political and economic processes through which we live and resist. Yet as Munshi and Willse (2017) argue, it is important to differentiate between structures, form and content. Both the prison industrial complex and its military predecessor are regimes of violence, explicitly functioning to repress dissent. The non-profit model manages and controls dissent by incorporating it into the state apparatus, operating as soft control to reinforce the direct control of the state. Critiques of the military and prison industrial complexes highlight the futility of reform and increasingly call for the abolition of systems of violent oppression. In contrast, there are many features to be saved and nurtured within the non-profit space, where lifesaving resources are distributed, leadership skills are developed and shared, and communities are established.

As the Incite! anthology demonstrates, moving beyond the restrictions and confines of the non-profit industrial complex involves thinking about the independent modes of social organisation available. The non-profit sector remains a site through which workers, volunteers, activists and community members 'collaboratively transform the conditions of everyday life' (Munshi and Willse 2017, p.xx). The PRA model demonstrates this through a continued commitment to working collaboratively with prisoners and partner organisations. The pressures and restrictions of the sector lead to inward-looking, niche operations which compete with each other and lose sight of their initial aims (Smith 2017). Instead, prison radio provides a platform for non-profits to work together to promote their services; placing prisoners at the centre of developing and producing relevant and engaging radio ensures ongoing PRA accountability to their primary stakeholders.

Discussion of the current status of the non-profit sector highlights contemporary restrictions and opportunities in the fight for welfarism and change. Equally, the establishment of the PRA needs to be understood within the unique historical context of 'Third Way' politics. The New Labour landslide election victory of 1997 provides the backdrop for UK prison radio growth. The PRA epitomises the Third Way communitarian approach to social justice and the repositioning of the voluntary sector in social welfare provision. Widely attributed to Anthony Giddens (1998) and developed by Tony Blair's New Labour, the Third Way describes a middle ground between the top-down, society-focused, welfare state and the market-driven, self-determining individualism of neoliberalism (Rose 2000). Individual responsibility and economic productivity are combined with notions of social justice and renewed focus on community and collective responsibility.

The PRA is a product of an environment in which the third sector was formalised, yet such strategies equally represent governmental techniques for diluting the campaigning and oppositional potential of the sector and bureaucratising smaller organisations out of existence. Many non-profit organisations struggled to negotiate a shifting funding landscape based on cooperative working with inflexible and bureaucratic government agencies. Similarly, the comparable institutional changes in the still largely public sector agencies of HM Prison Service and the BBC contributed to the key partnerships that PRA founders describe as pivotal to the organisation's development. Growing from a single project at this time, they were in a unique position to flexibly adapt their operations to fit within the institutional structures of partner organisations while striving to maintain independence, autonomy and focus on their core objectives.

With the emergence of a new breed of professionalised, well-funded and well-organised organisations, John Morison highlights developing tensions between the professional, managerial approach and a more traditional, informal, volunteering ethos. A rise in economic rationality, including the move towards managerialism, and an emphasis on efficiency and business practice, puts more traditional ideas of social welfare at risk (Morison, 2000, p.109). The conflict between social aims and professionalism can be seen through similar patterns within the community media sector, where a focus on professionalism and the highest broadcast standards possible is often seen in opposition to the primary aim of promoting access, participation, diversity and plurality (Van Vuuren 2001).

Writing on the changing role of the volunteers and voluntary agencies in prisons in 2002, PRA co-founder and Chair Roma Hooper also highlights the dangers of managerialism and over-regulation. Volunteers in prison have long been involved with supporting prisoners and their families, yet voluntary agencies had remained largely invisible to the Prison Service and individual establishments (Bryans et al 2002, p.13). Hooper (2002, p.103) identifies a shift in the acknowledgement of the role of prison volunteers in the early 2000s, illustrated through the creation of the new position of Voluntary Sector Co-ordinator for the Prison Service and a good practice guide for governors and agencies produced by Clinks, the umbrella organisation for supporting and representing volunteers in prison. While calling for a cohesive strategy of joint initiatives between voluntary agencies and prisons, she stresses the importance of the continued independence of the sector. 'Working together' does not equate with becoming totally absorbed within the prison culture and methods. Instead, the quality and strength of volunteers and voluntary organisations lies in their alternative perspective and independent culture:

> To over-managerialise them could not only be demotivating but deny them the most important quality they have – a non-statutory, experienced, confidential and caring listening ear which transcends the institutional setting and enables the prisoners and their families to benefit from service and support which they may not be able to access elsewhere. (Hooper 2002, p.104)

The voluntary sector qualities outlined by Hooper illustrate the principles on which the PRA was founded. Rapid shifts in third sector policy and practice set the scene for the growth of the PRA within the political context of the late 1990s and early 2000s. The Third Way placed the voluntary sector at the centre of welfare reform, offering a solution to the civic decay of Thatcher's Britain based on a commitment to civil society and the generation of social capital. Yet equally, the reworking of social aims in managerialist and economic terms represents an extension of neoliberalism, harnessing and developing the market potential of social and voluntary action. The PRA story is one of balance, relating to the wider opportunities and challenges of the non-profit sector, and the ability to navigate a new funding and operational environment while retaining independence in order to achieve the aims of supporting and representing prisoners.

Social activism, volunteerism and entrepreneurship

Where the above discussion outlines the political and economic shifts which have repositioned the work of the broader sector, similar changes have reframed the role of the volunteers, activists and workers who continue to provide vital services and campaign for social change. The prison radio story spans from the first voluntary radio broadcast within HMYOI Feltham, to the establishment of the PRA as a registered charity, the launch of flagship station Electric Radio Brixton, and the beginnings of NPR. There is a clear distinction between those involved at each stage, from early volunteer founders with little or no prior radio experience, to paid professional radio practitioners. However, individual accounts show a collection of complementary skills, combined to varying degrees, and developed through a range of professional backgrounds, primarily those of community development, criminal justice, education, social work and public service broadcasting. The combination of these skills and backgrounds not only highlights a common set of social, non-commercial values, but demonstrates an ethical commitment to non-profit and public sector working that has helped to define the organisation's activity and shape its development.

Radio Feltham began in the early 1990s, before the emergence of Third Way policy and the formalisation of the third sector. Instead, it grew out of the self-organisation of individual volunteers who were concerned about the rise of self-inflicted deaths in youth custody in their local community and felt that radio could help. The volunteer founders remain involved in prison radio as PRA Chair and Company Secretary, yet they came to the field with limited prior involvement or experience in broadcasting. They were concerned with addressing a particular social problem in whatever way they felt would make the most impact. The beginning of Radio Feltham was primarily un-funded, driven by those who identified a social need and potential solution, and reliant on those who had the passion, skill and commitment and time to make it happen. Later development sees the formal establishment of the PRA with paid staff, business and strategic planning, and government contracts. Where theories of volunteerism and social activism can be applied to early prison radio activity, later growth demonstrates the merging of these themes with a discourse of entrepreneurship and enterprise that has redefined both the media industry and social welfare practice.

From the outset, the prison radio concept demonstrates the overlapping characteristics of volunteerism and social activism. In 1992, now PRA Company Secretary Mark Robinson read a plea for help in the press from the local prison following a series of five youth suicides in quick succession. Feeling that prison radio could work in much the same way as the more established format of hospital radio in promoting communication and combating feelings of isolation, he enlisted the help of his friend and neighbour, Roma Hooper, now PRA Chair (Robinson 2012). Hooper had significant experience of fundraising in the disability sector which not only indicates the specific skills to raise money to start a project, and experience of navigating public and charitable sector systems, but a commitment to social inclusion that characterises social activism, whether paid or unpaid.

Volunteerism is notoriously difficult to define due to the range of activities that the term encompasses, from prison visiting to producing community radio. An understanding of what motivates people to give their time and skills to benefit others is equally hard to achieve due to the vast array of personal, political and cultural beliefs and values that underpin such actions. However, there has been a rapid increase in the study of volunteering over the past 25 years, originally prompted by a growing concern over the provision of social services in an age of increasing materialism and individualism (Wilson 2000, p.233) and more recently, in an attempt to inform wider sector development. Writing on the contribution of volunteers in the penal system, Hooper (2002, p.92) identifies a tendency for the actions of volunteers to be confused with those of the wider voluntary sector. Instead, she defines volunteering as 'unpaid (except for out-of-pocket expenses); freely chosen; done through the medium of an organisation or agency; and for the benefit of others or the environment as well as oneself' (Hooper 2002, p.12)

Where volunteers seek to help society, activists aim to change society. However, the accounts of PRA participants relate to both positions, focused on supporting prisoners while changing attitudes about prison and rehabilitation. The roots of the PRA lie in the desire to address the individual problem of suicides in custody at HMYOI Feltham, yet the growth of the activity and the organisation's focus on the potential for wider social change around the treatment of prisoners, demonstrates that the terms 'volunteerism' and 'social activism' in this instance are not only closely related, but can be interchangeable.

This merging of the terms is supported by John Wilson, who argues that the two roles are social constructions which need to be examined in conjunction with each other (2000, p.217). Where there is a case for distinguishing between activism and volunteerism along the lines of the different types of people they attract, social circumstances help to determine the meaning of the two roles and their relationship to each other. Using the example of the AIDS crisis, Wilson shows that when the government was slow to respond, volunteers doubled up as activists to deal with the problem (2000). This is further demonstrated in relation to the significance of volunteer organisations in prison, with a report by Clinks highlighting the continued role the voluntary sector plays in addressing social problems. They argue that rather than merely providing prisoner services, there is a diverse range of assets that set volunteer organisations apart from other sectors: 'they are advocates, campaigners, sources of vital information on service user need, a critical eye on existing services, and innovators that drive service change' (Clinks 2014, p.3).

As Wojciech Sokolowski (1996) demonstrates, the understanding of why people volunteer is informed by both personal motives, attitudes and dispositions, and the influence of social ties and interaction on the individual actor. Building on the study of social movements and civil rights activism (McAdam

1986), he highlights the similarities between what he describes as 'philanthropic activism' and involvement in social movements. Both behaviours are forms of collective action requiring the interaction and cooperation of a group of people, and both aim to achieve some form of social good requiring a degree of personal commitment as well as spontaneity, dedication and orientation towards others (Sokolowski 1996, p.262).

What drew Robinson and Hooper to prison radio is explained through social ties and interaction based on shared ideologies and social goals. Both refer to becoming involved through neighbours and friends, of enlisting the help of their wider network of contacts in gaining support for the project, and of the bonds that developed with people working within the prison. As Sokolowski (1996) highlights, people engage in philanthropic activities through social or organisational affiliations. Once engaged, there is a snowball effect of participation which impacts on individual attitudes and values, and ultimately motivates people towards further activity and a desire to pursue the 'next worthy deed' (Sokolowski 1996, p.275). Hoping to take a break from fundraising, Hooper (2012) needed some persuading to commit to the fundraising role again but admits to "being hooked" from her first visit to the prison, struck by the people who cared inside, and the lack of awareness about prisons on the outside.

Discussion of the motivations and drivers behind setting up a prison radio project demonstrates the interdependent relationship between personal and collective values that form the basis of social action. Interviews with Chief Executive Phil Maguire, Trustee and founding Chair Kieron Tilley, and current Director of Radio and Operations Andrew Wilkie all demonstrate the same values and social objectives of the volunteer founders, together with talk of being drawn to the opportunity, of a unique and powerful idea, and the potential to drive it forward. Their accounts typify the commitment, values and innovation attributed to a new breed of socially motivated ethical entrepreneur championed throughout Third Way policy. Yet the political and discursive repositioning of 'entrepreneurship' is problematic, representing the neoliberal governmental appropriation of volunteer and activist principles. Where founders exhibit the economic qualities of enterprise and entrepreneurship, their accounts remain firmly based in the social objectives of producing quality radio to improve the lives of prisoners.

The development of prison radio beyond Radio Feltham can be traced to a BBC partnership project examined further in Chapter Four. Here the story illustrates the individual backgrounds and aims of the founding staff members. Following a number of meetings with various BBC figures, Hooper (2012) describes the contact with Keith Beech, Managing Editor of BBC West Midlands, as the point "where it all started", stressing the importance of finding the right person to take it forward. Beech helped to bring together a steering group comprising of the Prison Service, Probation Service, education providers and the BBC, while Hooper speedily established charitable status and put together a small Board chaired by Tilley, then Head of Learning for BBC Radio (Hooper 2012). In September 2005, Maguire was seconded as BBC Prison Radio Co-ordinator to focus full time on development. From this point, the PRA grew beyond its volunteer roots, gradually building a team of paid, specialist staff able to dedicate the additional time and energy to develop prison radio.

Within one year, two new prison radio stations were established, radio skills training courses were delivered, the PRA was officially launched with a high profile event at HMP Birmingham, and Maguire left the BBC to become the organisation's first Chief Executive. The momentum continued into the following year with the development of a regional pilot project involving six additional prisons, the beginnings of Electric Radio Brixton, and Tilley leaving the BBC to become the PRA Director of Operations.

Both Tilley and Maguire talk of their moves from the BBC to the PRA as a logical next step, combining their previous skills, experience and personal values with a new and exciting opportunity. Tilley was linked to Radio Feltham in the late 1990s through a previous role as Regional Manager of non-profit organisation CSV Media, a connection that eventually led to my own involvement. Having identified potential staff and part-funding for a training course within the prison, he talks of his frustration when the project fell through at the last hurdle for funding reasons, and his continued interest in the idea when it reappeared during his later involvement with the BBC Corporate Social Responsibility Steering Group (Tilley 2012). Maguire's background also illustrates this pattern: after his time as a residential social worker in a children's home and teaching children excluded from school, he retrained as a broadcast journalist and was working as a producer for BBC Radio 2 when he saw the prison radio opportunity, describing it as bringing his different interests together, "radio and doing something positive" (Maguire 2012).

Reflecting on their individual motivations for moving from the BBC, both accounts are framed in voluntary and public sector discourse of a desire to 'make a difference' and do something 'important' while equally demonstrating the innovation and enterprise of the private sector through talk of 'risk', 'opportunity' and 'potential' (Maguire 2012; Tilley 2012). Both remain committed to the public service ethos, yet the BBC's shift towards a more enterprising model of Public Service Broadcasting ironically contributed to their decisions to leave to be entrepreneurial in their own right, with the freedom to shape something new in their own way.

Tilley in particular talks of his frustration with BBC bureaucracy restricting creativity, with clearance for every decision needed even when working at a relatively high level. As Head of Learning for BBC Radio, and with involvement with CSR outreach, he had the job he thought he "had always wanted", but he talks of being "unfulfilled" and not being used as creatively as possible (Tilley, 2012). Tilley was already in post as Chair of the inaugural PRA Board on a voluntary basis and describes the decision to leave the BBC to focus full time on PRA development as "an opportunity ... to make a real difference". Equally, he recognised the risk of leaving a job at the BBC to work for small start-up charity, with only one year of confirmed funding, "It was a gamble ... we didn't know whether a national project would ever get off the ground, but it was something we thought could be *really* exciting" (Tilley 2012).

The excitement and enthusiasm for what both Tilley and Maguire identify as the potential of prison radio typify the commitment, values and creativity of those developing innovative projects and services within the public and creative sectors. With their small start-up media organisation focused on developing a quality radio service for a previously unrecognised, niche, target audience, PRA founders are representative of the independent, 'cultural entrepreneurs' reshaping the creative industries. Equally, contributing to a small start-up non-profit organisation developing an innovative, client-centred service within the public sector, their experiences reflect those of the 'social entrepreneurs' credited as redefining public and voluntary sector practice.

Charles Leadbeater's work on social and cultural entrepreneurship in the late 1990s represents New Labour's policy position, reframing free market development in social and communitarian terms. Both the *Rise of the Social Entrepreneur* (1997) and *Why Cultural Entrepreneurs Matter* (Leadbeater and Oakley 1999) were published by Demos, the cross party thinktank closely aligned to New Labour in the run up to the election victory and recognised as helping to develop the party vision. As an advisor to Blair's government, Leadbeater presents entrepreneurship as central to social and economic reform, simultaneously informing and justifying government policy and rhetoric. It is a political repositioning which successfully co-opts the creativity and innovation of independent endeavours, representing governmental control of social action and cultural production.

The main contention is in the reworking of the term 'entrepreneur', formalising a connection between social and cultural innovation and capitalistic, profit-making motivations. This is particularly prominent in Leadbeater and Oakley's (1999) argument on the significance of cultural entrepreneurs, recognising their role in replacing declining manufacturing industries through the growth of the knowledge-based economy. They equate the term 'cultural entrepreneurs' with 'The Independents', or the small, independent operations involved with the production and distribution of cultural products, from band promoters, to graphic designers, music producers and freelance journalists. The rise of the independent is linked to shifts in the wider creative industries, enabled through the rapid pace of technological change and reacting to the domination of global media corporations. Leadbeater and Oakley define the cultural entrepreneur as the product of a convergence of the three forces of technology, values and economics (2005, p.302), all of which fit comfortably with the accounts of PRA founders. From a technology perspective, they are enabled rather than threatened by advances in digital radio production and distribution techniques. They are characterised by common values which are 'anti-establishment and anti-traditionalist' and prioritise choice, freedom, and autonomy, predisposing them to 'pursue self-employment and entrepreneurship in a spirit of self-exploration and self-fulfilment' (Leadbeater and Oakley 2005, p.302).

Equally, economic conditions have contributed to a move towards more independent working, as demonstrated through Tilley and Maguire's decision to leave the BBC. The rise of the independent workforce is a reaction to increased job insecurities since the late 1980s, with careers in large organisations becoming more uncertain (Leadbeater and Oakley 2005, p.302). While both were in secure jobs at the BBC, the restructuring and downsizing of the organisation contributed to the increasing relevance of independent working as a realistic and attractive option.

Leadbeater and Oakley (1999) highlight the positivity of new models of working within the creative industries, calling for policy development to support cultural entrepreneurs. However, the difficulty lies in the focus on economic value, citing profit and growth as the primary motivation, and advice including, 'Don't aim to become the next Bill Gates, aim to get bought out by him' (Leadbeater and Oakley 2005, p.310). Creative industries commentators argue that the success of the cultural entrepreneur is measured by economic growth and profit (Leadbeater and Oakley 1999; Hesmondhalgh 2002; Howkins 2002). Yet it is a position that fails to acknowledge the array of motivations and values behind any creative mission. As shown through the PRA story, what motivates innovators of any kind is not profit, but a passion for what they do, which creates the necessary energy, creativity and inspiration to drive projects forward. More than profit, the ability to act independently, according to individual values and beliefs fosters greater creativity and success.

Summary

This chapter has focused on the people behind the PRA, highlighting the values and motivations behind the formation of prison radio. Considering the PRA in the context of the wider non-profit sector, I introduced the contradictory forces that have redefined volunteerism, social activism and cultural production in recent decades. The establishment and expansion of the PRA reflects the governmental repositioning of the non-profit sector in rebuilding a framework for social care. Similarly, the place of the PRA within the wider broadcast sector indicates the recognition of independent media production as central to the growth of creative industries. Within this context, the formalisation of prison radio from a volunteer project to a national organisation, working in partnership with state, voluntary and private sector organisations, epitomises emerging strategies for social and welfare reform.

The establishment of prison radio is representative of new opportunities for social innovation. Equally, discussion of the historical Third Way UK political context from which the PRA emerged, and the contemporary expansion of the non-profit industrial complex through which it continues to evolve, demonstrates the challenges faced by those trying to enact change within an increasingly restrictive, managerialised and corporatised sector. Neoliberal discourse and policy reframe social action through a focus on the 'value' of social and cultural 'entrepreneurship', appropriating volunteerism and social activism through a process which not only harnesses potential impact but restricts the innovation and creativity that define it. Where this often leads to organisations losing sight of their initial aims as they struggle to survive, the accounts of PRA founders show a continuation of shared aims and values, committed to remaining accountable to the prisoner audience, and working collaboratively with partners.

Through discussion of the literature relating to the political and cultural context of broadcasting, prisons and voluntary sector in the preceding chapters, I have identified common themes around the contradictory, yet interdependent, relationship between the formal structures of government and state, and informal, community-based social action. This highlights the unique positioning of the PRA, representing a bridge between state and civil society. In the following section, I focus on key examples that demonstrate the ways in which the PRA navigated the process, balancing governmental and institutional opportunities and restrictions while remaining focused on social change to improve the lives of prisoners.

PART II

Prison Radio Association Case Studies

4

Rethinking Public Service Broadcasting: The PRA and the BBC

In Part I, I outlined some of the key theories useful for informing the understanding of prison radio. Here, these ideas are used to examine the information gathered through interviews with PRA participants on their experiences of the earliest stages of prison radio development. The findings are presented in a broadly chronological order, beginning with the events immediately prior to the formation of the PRA. Rather than a purely historical analysis, the following chapters are structured around prominent discursive themes identified through the accounts: namely, the partnerships and institutional arrangements involved; and the management of perceptions and assumptions about prison radio which have influenced the process. Two case studies are used to illustrate each theme, starting with the partnership arrangements which contributed to the early growth of prison radio and shaped the development of the PRA.

This chapter focuses on a partnership project in the West Midlands region which developed prison radio beyond Radio Feltham. In particular, I examine the role of the BBC in the process and the impact of the activity on establishing and formalising the PRA. Developed through the combined influence of national broadcaster and independent prison radio activity, I argue that the PRA is representative of new forms of Public Service Broadcasting (PSB) within changing media and institutional environments, achieved in partnership, and demonstrating the enduring importance of PSB values.

The role, function and legitimacy of PSB is under threat, shown through well-documented changes in BBC culture and operations (Born 2003, 2004) within an increasingly fragmented, commercialised and digitised media landscape. Examined against a backdrop of institutional changes throughout the 1990s and 2000s, BBC involvement with prison radio is linked to renewed corporate objectives of accountability, diversity and social responsibility in the face of an ongoing need to justify public funding. However, as an independent enterprise working in partnership with state agencies, the PRA represents the innovative and accountable community engagement to which the BBC aspired. Evolving as a small, independent social enterprise, the PRA epitomises the innovation, creativity and public service values which the BBC was arguably struggling to achieve (Born 2004).

The ways in which PRA founders tell their stories informs the understanding of prison radio growth. 'People', 'relationships', and 'partnerships' emerge as prominent themes throughout these accounts, with a number of relationships discussed as playing a major role and continuing to be an important feature of current activity. 'Partnership' appears as a key term throughout the accounts of the early stages, with recollections of relationships with particular personalities, and the balance of retaining independence appearing as recurring themes. The PRA is discussed as a 'conduit', facilitating relationships with diverse stakeholders in order to develop and create radio made by and for prisoners.

Collaborative working continues to be a fundamental feature of effective prison radio functioning, bringing together and representing the often conflicting needs of different groups. The ongoing PRA partnership with the Ministry of Justice is the ideal illustration of the process, based on over ten years of relationship building in order to plan, roll out and broadcast National Prison Radio. A dedicated Head of Prison Radio is employed through the department's executive agency, Her Majesty's Prison and

Probation Service, and bi-monthly governance meetings with the PRA ensure an ongoing dialogue and collective approach to addressing issues such as infrastructure and networking upgrades.

Equally, building and maintaining a relationship with prisoners is critical. Ongoing and meaningful audience engagement is essential for the authentic representation of prisoner issues, achieved through encouraging listener feedback and prioritising prisoner involvement in the production process. This is combined with building relationships with staff at individual prisons to facilitate the practicalities of radio production and broadcast. The ability to support radio training and develop content creation in different prisons is essential for the delivery of a service that represents the interests of prisoners from around the country. For instance, 'Hindley Young Persons' Entertainment', or HYPE for short, is a weekly NPR show produced at a Young Offender Institution in Manchester, addressing the specific challenges faced by young people in prison. Content development is equally dependent on working with the range of non-profit service providers involved in supporting people in prison, with the PRA partnering with 147 organisations in 2016 alone (PRA 2017b).

Developing throughout the late 1990s and 2000s, the PRA's aims and achievements connect to a policy shift towards intersectoral 'partnership working'. Rather than a conscious tactic, PRA participants describe an organic process based on personal relationships and shared aims and values. From the initial activity at Radio Feltham, PRA founders were able to build on the ways in which the idea aligned with cultural, policy and institutional objectives of the time, developing and shaping prison to fit with the needs of multiple stakeholders while retaining independence.

The reworking of the meaning and function of 'partnership' is a neoliberal strategy central to the expansion of the prison and non-profit industrial complexes. Instead of indicating collaborative working, the discursive repositioning of the term is used to justify and further the privatisation of public services. Norman Fairclough's analysis of the language of New Labour demonstrates the prominence of the term in contemporary political discourse and policy, indicative of governmental efforts to restructure public sector practice (2000). Increased opportunities for public, private and non-profit sector partnership working may well suggest increased autonomy and collaboration in the delivery of social welfare. Yet as Fairclough argues (2000, p.127), the shift merely represents a repackaging of Thatcher era privatisation strategies in less threatening, more communitarian language.

Where public service and social welfare are reframed in economic terms, 'partnership' discourse functions as a technology of control rather than an opportunity for development. Across the public, private and non-profit sectors, organisations are required to demonstrate intersectoral arrangements in order to access funding. In an increasingly competitive and under-resourced environment, partnerships then become linked to economic survival. Rather than fostering collaboration to develop holistic service delivery, the process can detract from the initial aims, inhibiting social innovation. In contrast, PRA partnership discourse focuses on the importance of personal relationships, describing prison radio as built on the principles of mutual support and collaboration.

The evolution of the PRA is a model of partnership working, representing what Fairclough describes a 'new 'networked' form of governance' (2000, p.124). Equally, the ability to successfully negotiate and manage the needs and aspirations of partners remains central to the organisation's function and development. Recognising both the opportunities and challenges, the need to manage and maintain a balance between different stakeholder objectives is a recurrent theme. Far from unique to prison radio, these challenges are typical of emerging arrangements. As Fairclough argues, the sustainability of networks based on diverse interests and agendas is questionable, with marked differences between the model and aspiration, and the 'messier realities' (2000, p.124). In building an authentic service, made for and by prisoners, success lies in the ability to navigate such a complex process while maintaining independence and focus.

Building a relationship with the BBC marks a pivotal point in the expansion of prison radio and establishment of the PRA. Founders talk of the 'crucial' role the partnership played in kickstarting the growth of activity, contributing both practical support and credibility to the project. While there are other equally significant partnerships which continue to support and influence the PRA, it is a relationship that warrants further examination within the context of rapid change and reconfiguration of broadcasting during the period.

The BBC Prison Radio Partnership

Hooper describes a visit to Radio Feltham in 2002 as marking the beginnings of BBC recognition of prison radio. She describes the reaction of BBC Radio 2 legal representative Andrew Phillips, claiming she should be "bottling this and getting it out" and encouraging her to write to the then Director-General, Greg Dyke, with a wish list for developing prison radio (Hooper, 2012). Hooper's request for help was passed on to Michael Hastings, then Head of Corporate Social Responsibility (CSR) and soon to be Director-General from 2004 to 2012. Hastings visited Radio Feltham together with the Head of BBC Radio 1, meeting with the governor to discuss the possibility of work experience opportunities for prisoners. Phillips continued to network, connecting Hooper to interested contacts at BBC West Midlands where she describes a two-year lead up, from the initial suggestion to finding the right people to form a regional steering group to develop prison radio further.

PRA Trustee, founding Chair and former Director of Operations Kieron Tilley was Head of Learning for BBC Radio at the time, a role combining community outreach with staff development. He recalls the subject of prison radio being raised by Hastings at a BBC CSR Reporting Steering Group meeting, "and I couldn't put my hand up quick enough" (Tilley, 2012), seeing it as an opportunity to support a project that he had hoped to develop at Radio Feltham through his previous role as CSV Media South East Regional Manager years earlier. Tilley was central to establishing the regional steering group and later launching the PRA, with his BBC role not only providing specialist knowledge and contacts within the corporation but also bringing credibility and legitimacy to the project. As PRA Chief Executive, Maguire (2012) reflects, "I think that the fact that the BBC were taking this partnership seriously meant that everyone else did".

Tilley and Hooper networked with a range of stakeholders within the region, including representatives from the Prison Service, Probation Service, regional BBC, further education providers and voluntary sector groups. The group grew gradually from 2004, meeting regularly to discuss ideas and strategies for the development of a pilot project to test the viability of prison radio growth. Yet, while the group is described as 'enthusiastic', progress was slow until the BBC agreed to release a producer, through a BBC Training initiative, to develop the project. Tilley and Hooper prepared a job description and sat on an interview panel together with the BBC West Midlands Managing Editor, recruiting Maguire to the post of Prison Radio Co-ordinator in September 2005. Maguire moved from his position as producer and reporter on the BBC Radio 2 Jeremy Vine Show, successfully establishing two prison radio stations at HMP Birmingham and HMP Hewell over a nine-month period. Built around donated, decommissioned BBC analogue desks, the sound-proofed studios included mics, CD players and a computer with digital editing software, designed for training, recording and producing primarily speech-based content.

Combined with the ongoing commitment and enthusiasm of those involved, the rapid progress of the pilot project and increasing enquiries from other prisons, provided evidence that prison radio had the potential to develop further. As activity grew, Tilley and Hooper's idea of establishing a charitable organisation to continue the process began to take shape, and towards the end of his secondment term, Maguire started a conversation about leaving the BBC to become the first employee.

The PRA was officially launched at an event at HMP Birmingham in 2006, with the BBC covering the first three months of Maguire's salary as the organisation's inaugural Chief Executive, a degree of support that would be extremely unlikely within the current climate of staff and funding cuts. Tilley (2012) describes the relationship as remaining "hugely important" through links with BBC Outreach and the secondment of a Head of Prison Radio post to the then National Offender Management Service to work in partnership with the PRA on the roll-out of NPR. While a strong relationship continues, the start-up funding for Maguire's post marks the end of the BBC's direct contribution to the project, "after that, we were on our own two feet as the PRA" (Maguire 2012).

The BBC influence and impact on the PRA's organisational development reaches beyond that of formal partnerships and official support, continued through informal association and an ongoing pattern of BBC staff migrating to the PRA. After acting as inaugural PRA Chair of Trustees, Tilley made the controversial decision to give up his BBC post to focus on the charity, becoming PRA Director of Operations in 2007. A legacy continued with five of the key founding PRA staff moving from BBC positions and current NPR producers predominantly coming from BBC backgrounds. Far from indicative of a specific recruitment policy, both Maguire and Tilley attribute the trend to a focus on high quality speech-based production skills that remain almost exclusively within the BBC.

'There is a quality that we look for in the producers that we recruit, the producers that work for NPR and the PRA are at the top of their game. They are exceptional producers and they make exceptionally high quality speech content.' (Tilley 2012)

Throughout the reflections, 'ex-BBC staff' is coterminous with 'quality broadcasting', indicating a strong influence on the PRA's organisational and operational culture beyond the practicalities of specific funding and partnership arrangements. Without exception, PRA founders highlight the 'credibility', 'professionalism' and 'legitimacy' that the partnership afforded the project in the earliest stages, enabling them to attract funders and gain access to the prison system. In addition, BBC skills and experience continue to influence the PRA's broadcast model and production values, demonstrating the BBC's enduring reputation as a quality and trustworthy broadcaster within a context of public service reduction and a dramatically changing media environment.

The BBC context

Outlining a BBC crisis of legitimacy during the 1990s and early 2000s, Georgina Born connects the situation to the wider attack on public sector organisations, describing a process of privatisation and marketisation, with pressure to become competitive, commercial and therefore accountable, underpinned by the 'voracious growth of auditing' (Born, 2003, p.64). In *Uncertain Vision: Birt, Dyke and the Reinvention of the BBC* (2004) and associated works, Born's picture of the BBC at this time highlights the challenge of combining private sector business management techniques with the intangible nature of public services and the resulting negative impact on creativity. Under government pressure to demonstrate visible accountability, the BBC was restructured and redefined through a managerial discourse focused on performance targets and outputs. Again, the rise of public sector accountability is connected to the reforms of Thatcher's governments and the parallel ascendance of neoliberal values in public life. As Born describes (2003, p.65), converging forces throughout the 1980s and early 1990s created a new managerialism, which resulted in a crisis of both funding and legitimisation of the BBC.

The involvement of the BBC in prison radio development needs to be examined from this context of crisis and change, as the corporation struggled to demonstrate relevance and value against criticisms of London-centric elitism by introducing initiatives such as 'Open Learning Centres' and 'Local TV' that expanded the focus on accessibility and diversity beyond the act of making programmes. Rather than dismissing the Reithian principles on which the BBC was based, a new form of corporate ethics added to the equation as the BBC attempted to expand the engagement of staff outside programme making and services. This is exemplified through both the existence and status of the CSR Board within the corporation, and staff positions including Tilley's then role, both of which were fundamental drivers in the development of the prison radio partnership.

The BBC staff development and outreach initiatives that facilitated Tilley and Maguire's involvement with prison radio represent the development of a new corporate ethic, while equally contributing to their decision to move away. Both acknowledge their ongoing respect for the BBC as the epitome of quality broadcasting yet discuss their motivations for leaving as based on a need for creative freedom combined with a desire to do something 'worthwhile' and 'important' (Maguire 2012; Tilley 2012). Within the context of new managerial policies of the 1990s and early 2000s, Born (2003) presents the BBC as stuck between systematic auditing and accountability on one hand, and quasi-markets and entrepreneurialism on the other, resulting in negative consequences for the core activity of programme making. Where creativity is restricted through managerialism and bureaucracy, the PRA as a start-up organisation growing independently, from small yet focused beginnings, epitomises the freedom to innovate and adapt. In this case, the abstract principles of 'democracy, citizenship and universality' on which the BBC was formed (Born and Prosser 2001) are maintained, yet are rethought and achieved through creativity, independence and flexibility.

As Born shows (2003, p.64), the BBC was built on the Reithian vision of broadcasting as an instrument for social integration, for enhancing democratic functioning, and raising cultural and educational standards through the trinity of information, education and entertainment. It is a role which has long been central to the construction of national culture, mediating information and collective identities at the same time as inhabiting a space between public and private powers, state and people, propaganda and knowledge (Born 2003, p.64). In describing its unique status, Born presents the BBC as the combined ethical and cultural project of modern government with the Reithian ethic used as a practice of legitimation, 'through rhetorical displays of a sanctimonious soft nationalism, a nationalism that, in times of national crisis and celebration, the BBC claimed as its special territory' (2003, p.65).

However, as Elizabeth Jacka (2003) argues, PSB is struggling to define itself as neoliberal political rationality moves away from the state. She argues that the automatic privileging of PSB output based on empty rhetoric of quality, democracy and citizenship no longer applies (2003, p.177). Yet, where Jacka renders PSB obsolete, the PRA represents a new model based on reworked and enduring ideals in a new media environment. PSB is struggling to adapt and respond to rapid changes in communications contexts, 'under attack' around the world; where PSB is threatened, Jacka describes a 'veritable avalanche of discourse' attempting to defend its existence: 'Key concepts are intoned like mantras – public service, public sphere, citizenship, democracy – as if by their repetition alone they had the power to persuade unwilling governments to continue to support PSB' (2003, p.178).

When discussing the origins of prison radio, PRA founders highlight the democratic function of radio, demonstrating a belief in the power of radio to 'give people a voice', empowering and informing minority groups through information and representation, with activity based on the principles of public service and citizenship that are used to defend the continued role of traditional PSB. Yet Jacka (2003, p.182) challenges the assumption that PSB contributes to democracy in any way, critiquing contemporary theories of democracy as failing to reflect the complex and changing nature of citizenship in a pluralised society. Again, the concept of radical democracy (Mouffe 1992) is used to highlight the reworking of ideas of citizenship and democracy beyond a social contract with the state towards associational networks of civil society, where people make smaller decisions that to some degree shape, 'the more distant determinations of state and economy' (Jacka 2003, p.182).

The PRA demonstrates the enduring democratic function of media, reclaiming and expanding PSB principles into a previously unexplored and unreached setting. Jacka's argument highlights the increasing complexity of both communication media and of democratic participation, recognising the need for 'a much more nuanced account of the connection between (various forms of) citizenship and the media' (2003, p.183). Where general arguments of 'specialness' have been replaced by free-market inspired arguments, there is a strong case for an individualised approach to the discussion of PSB that goes beyond the automatically privileging of 'high journalism' or mindless worship of populist media.

For Jacka, the concepts of democracy and citizenship have been reduced to the status of empty rhetoric used to defend an institution that is fundamentally undemocratic, representative of elitist, oppressive power. Yet where Jacka presents the defence of

PSB as resting on an 'essentialist conception of 'ideal democracy" (2003, p.181), David Nolan (2006) highlights the performative function of these concepts, applying Foucault's governmentality approach to show how institutions not only reflect, but create and produce definitions. PSB remains a technology of citizenship, with Nolan highlighting the role it performs in creating spaces where ideas of collective identity are articulated and deliberated. Recognising contemporary formations of citizenship as shaped by multiple interactions between authorities and publics, he argues that PSB informs modes of governmental practice and media practice that 'define' formations of citizenship rather than facilitating a notional ideal or abstract theorisation of it (Nolan 2006, p.227). PSB operates as a field of practice that works to 'performatively' define formations of citizenship, one that is simultaneously situated within, and governed by, a larger field of socio-political relations (Nolan 2006, p.228).

Referring to Paddy Scannell's portrayal of the role of the BBC in the formation of British public life (1989), Nolan argues that PSB not only produces citizenship, but defines citizenship through inclusion and exclusion, 'for different audience members, definitions of citizenship produced through broadcasting simultaneously work to produce forms of membership within, and exclusion from, the political community' (2006, p.230). Prison radio reconnects prisoners with citizenship, re-incorporating them into the political community and simultaneously serving to redefine formations of both prisoners and citizenship. Therefore, the BBC's role in this and similar community outreach initiatives should be seen as a reworking of the public service function, acting as agents of responsibilitisation within disenfranchised communities through the expansion of technologies of citizenship.

The citizen-forming role of the BBC has shifted dramatically over recent decades, with the prison radio relationship representing a drive to towards diversity, accessibility and audience accountability. The rise of neoliberal managerialism within the BBC documented by Born (2003, 2004) shows an institution in crisis as it strove to defend funding under the Conservative governments of the 1980s and 1990s. In line with the wider public sector, the BBC became subject to criticism.

> Public sector organisations were seen as unaccountable, inefficient, incompetent, self-serving and secretive. They were charged with being unresponsive to consumers and clients, of failing to offer consumer choice and – given the neoliberal equation of markets with democracy – of being undemocratic. (Born 2003, p.65)

Born describes the increasing condemnation of the BBC as excessively elitist and centralist in the context of the populist 1990s (2003, p.72). Instead, a discourse of consumer sovereignty was deployed and Director-General John Birt (1992–2000) transformed the corporation through New Public Management, characterised by audit and monitoring processes, and focused on measurable performance indicators (Born 2004, p.214): 'the effect is to render conceptually residual the questions of innovation, creativity, distinctiveness and quality that form the core of the BBC's public cultural remit' (Born 2003, p.72).

In addition, Born outlines the 'corrosive effects' of Birt's new managerialism on the culture of the BBC, 'stoking hierarchy and division' within the corporation (2004, p.215). Under the New Labour governments, Birt's successors, Greg Dyke and Mark Thompson, strove to rebuild staff morale and introduced initiatives that built on the public duty of the BBC as reflecting and responding to the needs of audiences. The increased focus on social responsibility and community outreach that the prison radio partnership represents can be seen as a reaction against the inward-facing bureaucratic BBC culture of the 1990s. As Hooper (2012) recalls, the status and influence of the CSR Board within the corporation at the time was a major contributor to the growth of prison radio, and the project sat well with a BBC drive towards greater diversity and audience accountability in the face of criticisms of elitism.

Evolving PSB

When asked why they felt the BBC became involved in the project, PRA founders outline multiple factors including community benefit, reaching a new audience, producing new content and staff development opportunities. Maguire maintains that the desire to do something positive within the local community was a big driver for the initial involvement of BBC West Midlands. He equally recognises the rationale behind the funding of the Prison Radio Co-ordinator post as based on the ability to produce new and engaging content from and about prisons. Tilley and Maguire describe staff development opportunities as a major factor in the process. Through placing BBC staff with community groups, they were able to provide specialist skills while learning about partnership working with other groups and agencies and gaining valuable insight into audiences (Maguire 2012). For both, this connects to the importance of what Tilley (2012) describes as the BBC's 'public purpose' of reaching diverse audiences, with prisoners recognised as among the hardest to reach.

The BBC focus on staff development opportunities within communities indicates a desire to reconnect with audiences and justify the public service function. The ability to cater for minority groups is a traditional defence of PSB, yet automatic assumptions about the effectiveness and relevance of services are invalid in a new media environment with a rapidly expanding diversity of platforms and content. While audiences are increasingly dispersed, PSB supporters continue to argue the need for universally accessible, free-to-air services with a range of content that reflects cultural diversity and fosters social cohesion and inclusion (Harrison and Wessels 2005, p.835).

A key distinction here is the relevance of traditional PSB models and values for minority audiences. Where the reputation of the BBC is recognised as a major factor in developing the partnerships on which the PRA was built; independence and grassroots credibility are described as equally important. The activity grew through a unique selection of relationships and arrangements which combined the top-down national broadcaster role aiming to engage with diverse audiences in new ways with that of grassroots media activism committed to serving the needs of prisoners. Rather than the BBC alone, it is the partnership model that represents the expansion and reapplication of PSB values, creating relevant content by and with prisoners, a target audience that cannot be reached through traditional or emerging online media platforms.

The conditions that shaped and developed traditional PSB have been radically altered by technology, to the extent that government challenges to PSB funding and governance are somewhat justified. Jackie Harrison and Bridgette Wessels (2005) state that technological and institutional change are inextricably linked, arguing that PSB policy objectives are constrained by institutional arrangements that fail to enable audiences and users to shape and produce their own public service communications. Instead, they outline the new partnerships and alliances that are facilitating the use of new media and forming new ways of communicating, and show that developments in reconfiguring media remain based on the values of inclusion, participation and universal access.

Presenting a series of community ICT case studies from the early 2000s, Harrison and Wessels (2005) argue that such initiatives redefine the PSB ethos in a reconfigured new media environment. Their focus is on the use of free computer and internet access and activities designed to engage the public in urban regeneration, but the same can be applied to the case of community based media production projects at the time, with the regional prison radio partnership representative of changing institutional arrangements and new ways of communicating. Traditional PSB is formed through relationships between media institutions, their audiences, producers and funding, and shaped through statutory requirements imposed on them by their regulatory bodies. Yet new social relationships are emerging, with new technology enabling local grassroots activity and creating new forms of engagement.

The prison radio partnership is representative of the new relationships through which PSB is being redefined. However, while the BBC was influential in the process, the PRA could only flourish independently, outside institutional restrictions. Similarly, the emerging forms of PSB outlined by Harrison and Wessels are developed independently through partnership working and loose institutional frameworks which allow for experimentation with new forms of media 'in which public service values form the guidelines for development' (2005, p.836). In a digital media environment in which audiences are fragmented and dispersed across a rapidly increasing number of media platforms, the function of PSB also becomes dispersed and delivered through a range of relationships in which the BBC becomes one element. For instance, where the BBC brand added credibility to early activity, the support of the Ministry of Justice and individual prison governors is described as far more powerful and influential in the process.

Rather than a formal arrangement with clearly defined roles and objectives, the prison radio steering group is discussed as a series of informal contacts and networks, evolving through shared personal and organisational aims. The flexibility to involve different partner organisations with complementary aims and identified skills represents a collective and responsive approach to development. This is illustrated through the example of CSV Media's role in identifying ways to combine activity with the delivery of accredited radio qualifications at HMPs Birmingham and Hewell (Maguire 2012). As Harrison and Wessels highlight, this organic growth is an essential feature of new technologies of partnership, functioning as a 'largely self-governing mode of operation' to respond to diverse interests and needs and develop a plurality of services and content (2005, p.836).

Their argument is useful for demonstrating the evolving and enduring characteristics of PSB within a reconfigured media environment, particularly how the PSB ethos is being redefined in ways that are completely separate from, and independent of, the BBC. Through arrangements that mirror features of the prison radio partnership, they describe the central role of non-media users and producers in the process, including public authorities and voluntary sector agencies. These arrangements build on issues of universal access, partnership and regulation, while also exploring citizenship, creativity, diversity and empowerment through participation, ultimately developing public service content tailored to local needs and produced through local democratic forums (2005, p.843). Arguably, the BBC is no longer central to the PSB model, where local partnerships and civil society organisations are more effective in ensuring diverse representations and responding to local needs. PSB as a technology of citizenship is now facilitated through emerging technologies of partnership with different groups, agencies and stakeholders. Therefore, the democratic role and function of PSB is no longer delivered by and for the state, but democratised and dispersed throughout civil society.

While effective partnership working is based on shared objectives and collaboration, the prison radio steering group involved additional challenges, combining and aligning the interests and aims of grassroots activism with those of the major institutional monoliths of the BBC and the Prison Service. For a small start-up charity, independence then becomes a risk, with PRA founders mindful of the point where institutional involvement becomes institutional control. Without exception, their accounts highlight the importance of independence if they were to remain credible with their target audience, determined to develop and retain a separate identity from the outset. The

BBC brand may have been instrumental in building trust and reputation with the Ministry of Justice, funders and partner agencies, yet PRA participants recognise independence as critical for building trust and retaining credibility with the prison audience, a point that equally applies to community based media projects that aim to support disadvantaged groups of any kind. This demonstrates that the PSB values of universality, access and citizenship are more effectively delivered through grassroots initiatives working in partnership with diverse audiences than through top-down institutional arrangements.

Summary

PRA founders describe the BBC partnership as a crucial element in the early development of the organisation, "without it, I don't think it would have happened" (Maguire 2012). The reputation of the BBC gave the project a credibility and gravitas that enabled them to gain trust and build relationships with other pivotal agencies and stakeholders. This is particularly relevant in the case of the Ministry of Justice whose often uneasy relationship with the media is explored further in Chapter Six. In addition, the provision of specialist staff not only helped to get the project off the ground through skills and funding, but set standards in quality production and organisational management which have continued to shape the PRA and development of NPR. However, the founding staff who migrated from the BBC describe the PRA as equally built on a freedom to innovate that was previously unavailable to them. As a start-up organisation, the PRA had the flexibility to adapt and respond to the multiple needs of diverse stakeholders in a way that large institutions are unable to.

In this chapter, I focused on the formation of a regional steering group and the role of the BBC in supporting and facilitating early prison radio. The partnerships and relationships forged during this period played a major role in the establishment and ongoing development of the PRA. The theme continues in Chapter Five through a case study of a second regional project, designed to test the feasibility and effectiveness of prison radio training. As the organisation's first formal contracted delivery, the education project not only expanded the PRA's work with prisoners and a range of new partners, but also provided the opportunity to demonstrate and evaluate the impact of prison radio.

5

Transformative Prison Education: The Prison Radio Training Project

Once formally established as a charity, the PRA successfully applied for a contract to design and trial the delivery of prison radio training packages in six prisons over six months in 2007 and 2008. As a project it is representative of the contemporary enterprise priorities of prison education, both in terms of the contractualisation of partnership projects and through a focus on employability skills and personal development opportunities for prisoners. Equally, the project is an example of the ways in which the PRA made the economic, cultural and political context work for them, able to justify and formalise activity through demonstrating outputs for the Prison Service and funding agencies, while using the process to develop and define the direction of the organisation.

While in post as BBC Prison Radio Co-ordinator, Maguire presents his role as "essentially micromanaging" the setup of two prison radio stations as well as responding to the growing number of enquiries from prisons around the country. The pilot enabled founders to identify a clear need to support prison radio stations, while at the same time realising that the ability to manage numerous projects was unsustainable (Maguire 2012). The capacity to trial models of delivery and identify opportunities shaped the direction and development of the PRA, achieved through consultation with a growing number of partner prisons and external organisations. The inaugural PRA Chair, Tilley (2012), outlines the initial aims of the charity as providing advice and guidance to existing and developing prison radio projects across the prison estate: "there were other pockets of prison radio activity across the country, but there was no single organisation that was showing best practice and networking each of these projects".

Immediately following the PRA's launch and Maguire's appointment as Chief Executive, the charity was primarily concerned with continuing the momentum and supporting prison radio stations. During this stage, two major projects emerged, with the organisation building on the activity in the West Midlands, as well as exploring possibilities at HMP Brixton in London. Led by the Learning and Skills Council (LSC), the West Midlands pilot was expanded through a regional project that resulted in the PRA's first formal partnership and government contract to test models of best practice in prison radio training.

In 2006, I moved from CSV Media to the PRA, joining as Education Director and becoming the second paid staff member. In a move that mirrors that of Maguire and Tilley's stories, my role came with a need to identify continued funding for the post and primarily involved securing and coordinating the prison radio training pilot. Facilitated through a contemporary policy focus on partnership working, innovation, enterprise and skills development, the project enabled the PRA as a start-up venture to trial services and build in an evaluation process to inform the organisation's strategic development. Both the project and the evaluation warrant further examination, indicative of shifting governmental techniques involved in the management and delivery of public services, including prison education.

The prison radio training pilot forms the basis of the evaluation of the organisation's first year, commissioned by the PRA and produced by the Sheffield Hallam University Centre for Community Justice (Wilkinson and Davidson 2008). Part of a three-year evaluation of the PRA's activities, the process was specifically designed to assess the extent to which the organisation met its objectives in order to demonstrate the potential benefits of prison radio (2008, p.11). The aim was to identify what worked well in terms of outputs and processes, and to provide information on progress in terms of objectives and the needs of key stakeholders, including prison inmates and staff. Designed and implemented in the earliest stages, the evaluation demonstrates the PRA's focus on organisational growth as well as recognising the importance of meeting the needs of a range of prison and external partners in the process.

The activity was funded through the last stages of the EQUAL strand of the European Structural Fund, designed to support innovative ways of tackling inequalities and discrimination in the labour market. In 2007, the LSC was the contract holder of £2 million of EQUAL funding for one year's activity in the West Midlands. Guided by the newly formed LSC Offender Learning and Skills Service (OLASS) division, the PRA, CSV, BBC and private training company Carter and Carter successfully applied for a subsidy arrangement by outlining a vocationally focused training project. Designed as a pilot scheme, the partnership aimed to develop a two-week taster course in radio production for delivery in six prisons across the region. Outlining the objectives, the evaluation report lists overall project delivery as well as the wider remit of examining the potential of radio training programmes within the Prison Service (Wilkinson and Davidson 2008, p.2).

The EQUAL framework and LSC OLASS guidelines emphasise the need to build on existing partnerships and formulate new ones, including relationships with additional prisons and Carter and Carter, a private training provider with a considerable foothold in prison education at the time. The funding application form itself asks for potential organisations to explicitly address the ways in which activity will demonstrate 'empowerment', 'innovation' and 'partnerships', while the project evaluation illustrates the recurrent link between the terms 'partnership', 'funding' and 'training' (Wilkinson and Davidson 2008, p.2). All are key words in neoliberal governmental discourse, implying the positive outcomes of new, collaborative initiatives for the beneficiaries, while equally loaded with economic connotations, indicative of the spread of enterprise culture, both in terms of how prisoners are considered and in how institutions operate. Prisoners are reimagined as rational economic actors, able to make choices and 'invest' in their own training and education, while the Prison Service is reconfigured around 'enterprising' partnership arrangements with private and voluntary sector service providers.

Larger, more established organisations struggled to adapt to new funding priorities and language, yet the PRA had the flexibility to work out ways in which the core activity of producing radio for prisoners could match with different funding and delivery options. For PRA founders, the project is seen as a learning experience, significant not only for demonstrating what prison radio could do, but in acknowledging the activities they felt were unsustainable. While the project was recognised as successful by the participants, partners and funders, it predicates the PRA's move away from direct education provision. Where courses were only able to reach small groups of prisoners at a time, focus shifted towards the wider impact of a National Prison Radio service, able to reach the entire prison population of over 80,000 people at any time.

For PRA founders, the main outcome of the project was the sharpening of this vision. Other organisational outcomes included the experience of negotiating and building new formal contract arrangements for a new and evolving organisation as well as providing the means for recruiting new staff, including my own role as Education Director, and former BBC broadcast journalist and Project Co-ordinator Jules McCarthy. The education focus also provided the opportunity to build a 'proven track record', demonstrating the impact of prison radio through the delivery of measurable outputs for potential partners and funders. Finally, the inclusion of an evaluation process not only satisfied funding requirements but significantly contributed to the PRA's ongoing strategic development by collating and presenting the first formal feedback from prisoners, prison managers, and partner organisations on the individual and institutional impact of prison radio.

Between September 2007 and February 2008, the PRA delivered an *Introduction to Radio Production* qualification through five two-week courses in four prisons. Building on activity at HMPs Birmingham and Hewell, the project was designed to expand to other prisons in the region. Heads of Learning and Skills at six prisons had originally expressed an interest in hosting courses, but the practicalities and short timescales for delivery resulted in the involvement of four: HMYOI Swinfen Hall; HMYOI Brinsford; HMP Long Lartin; with HMP Brockhill hosting a second two-week course.

Outlining the key findings of the evaluation, Wilkinson and Davidson highlight the impact on prisoners, with 24 learners successfully gaining an accredited qualification. Of the PRA learners who did not complete, three left due to early release, with only one learner failing to fulfil the course requirements (2008, p.22). Participants were interviewed at the start and end of the course, with feedback showing an increase in confidence and self-esteem. All learners reported that the course provided them with a positive educational experience that they were likely to repeat and they felt more confident about their options post-release (Wilkinson and Davidson, 2008, p.2). Overall, the successful qualification outcomes, positive learner feedback and prison staff observations contribute to the organisational objectives of demonstrating and promoting the potential of radio training for engaging prisoners in education as well as the wider significance of prison radio.

Creative learning

In a prison system where over half of the population has literacy levels below that expected of an 11 year old (Home Office

2004, p.17), the project was designed to reflect the priorities of the 'Education, Training and Employment' pathway of the newly published *Reducing Reoffending National Action Plan*. Recognising literacy and numeracy levels as a significant barrier to employment and long-term rehabilitation, the pathway aimed to increase basic and key skills among prisoners (Home Office 2004). Stakeholders saw radio as an effective and innovative way of engaging hard-to-reach offenders, and of providing a positive educational experience which would enhance basic skills and encourage prisoners back into further learning, "What we were looking for was something new, a way of engaging with people from the prison who potentially otherwise wouldn't engage and learn" (LSC Representative in Wilkinson and Davidson 2008, p.35).

The emphasis on basic and key skills relates to the 1995 introduction of the core curriculum, and resulting prison key performance targets to raise the number of prisoners with qualifications of Level Two and above (Clements 2004, p.173). By 2004, the curriculum had begun to reshape adult education both inside prison and out. Now rebranded under the more positive and affirming banner of *Skills for Life*, 'basic skills' focused on literacy, language and numeracy, while 'key skills' included the wider abilities of ICT, problem solving and working together, seen to underpin success in education, employment, lifelong learning and personal development.

Paul Clements' 2004 work on arts education in prisons is useful for understanding the contemporary effects of the adult education curriculum. Prison radio fits within an arts education framework, focusing on prisoner participation in the creative process. Yet Clements illustrates the hostile environment from which it emerged, claiming that by the early 2000s, the majority of arts provision had been 'replaced by an age of instrumental reason and measurement' (2004, p.173) through a short-term framework of skills targets. Outlining the need for a more creative and expressive curriculum, he shows a dramatic decline in opportunities for prisoners to engage with arts, replaced through a costly and ineffective move towards an instrumental agenda of basic, key and cognitive skills (Clements 2004, p.169).

Researching the changing role and curriculum of prison education over a five-year period, Clements found that, by 2001, arts classes at HMP Brixton had been reduced by 75%, with remaining provision reshaped to deliver elements of the basic and key skills curriculum, a pattern reflected across the prison estate (2004, p.173). Becoming governor of the prison in 2006, Paul McDowell (2012) too was struck by the negative culture and lack of activities for prisoners, placing the development of a radio station at the centre of a wider strategy to introduce more 'interesting' and creative initiatives. Clements' analysis fails to acknowledge the impact of the rapidly rising prison population on overcrowding and chronic lack of resources over this period, yet his work does highlight the inherent challenges of adapting and developing creative and empowering learning opportunities within a political and institutional framework based on performance targets.

The radio courses were designed to test ways of embedding basic and key skills delivery through engaging and creative learning. The evaluation found that all stakeholders felt that this was achieved in a way that would both encourage involvement in further learning and develop the skills that prisoners would need for employment on release. The majority of learners reported having difficult prior experiences of education and felt that they would be unlikely to enrol on a standard basic literacy course. On completion of the radio training, all acknowledged that their basic literacy skills had improved, as well as a range of wider skills including ICT; spelling; communication and public speaking; and working in a group (Wilkinson and Davidson 2008, p.35):

> I think all my skills have improved, it's all come together in this course. Radio just seems to have brought all my skills

together – this has been the best course I've ever been on.
(PRA Learners in Wilkinson and Davidson 2008, p.36)

Creative and arts education in prison focuses on the holistic development of individuals, rather than measurement of specific skills criteria. The radio project demonstrates the way that both approaches can be mutually supportive, achieving both institutional objectives and realising personal transformative potential. As Clements (2004) argues, arts programmes should support, not be an alternative to, the curriculum, a strategy that was beginning to emerge by the early stages of PRA development. Highlighting the lack of research in the field of prison education at the time, he outlines the range of different approaches for the examination of the arts, from practical and constructive use of time to behavioural and therapeutic effects, demonstrating both social and practical functions. Research conducted by early supporters of the PRA, the Anne Peaker Unit for Arts and Offenders, shows that engagement with creative programmes comes from 'a need to find a voice of their own in a situation where they have a few means of communicating with others and where they suffer a consequent loss of identity' (Clements 2004, p.172).

Falling between both educational and therapy frameworks, Clements argues that the arts instil confidence, challenge low esteem and assure prisoners that they are worth educating, becoming a vehicle through which can they can constructively occupy themselves and escape from the pressure of their immediate surroundings (2004, p.172). Creative programmes offer a far more effective reintroduction to lifelong learning than what he describes as 'dumbed down' basic skills, able to encourage a broader exploration of cultural values, individual behaviour and lifestyle by both 'emancipating and empowering the prisoner' (Clements 2004, p.174).

A discourse of empowerment and emancipation had begun to influence wider adult education practice by the late 1990s

(Inglis 1997). Radio production training in prisons aims to empower learners through communication skills, giving them a voice and helping them to express themselves, and therefore represent themselves, in their own terms. As a practical and creative activity, it contributes to both objectives, representing an attractive learning option for prisoners. However, the shifting meaning of 'empowerment' is problematic, becoming a key term in neoliberal governmental discourse, originating in the language of radical social movements of the 1960s, and gradually appropriated throughout education, social care, business, and organisational management.

A contemporary study of the adult education environment provides a useful illustration. Tom Inglis distinguishes 'empowerment' within the system from 'emancipation' as struggling for freedom by changing the system. Where emancipation involves critically analysing, resisting and challenging the systems of power, emphasis on personal empowerment focuses on the capacity for individual change. By highlighting the difference between the two concepts, he shows that a process leading to increased or devolved power also leads to a subtler form of incorporation (1997, p.3). A focus on reconstructing 'the self' through education foregrounds the potential for personal transformation while obscuring opportunities to challenge and confront the existing power structures (Inglis 1997, p.4). Therefore, the more emphasis on individual empowerment, the less likelihood there is of challenging and changing the dominant power structure and processes.

Inglis' work clearly outlines the issues of discipline and surveillance inherent in adult education policy and practice, demonstrating the extent to which emphasis on personal transformation has been reframed and repurposed as a means of social control (Inglis 1997, p.7). The argument is particularly relevant to the discussion of prison education where the power relationships and structures are even more visible and clearly defined. Where he suggests a pervasive and subtle form of control, prison education is explicitly concerned with shaping the behaviours of individuals both inside the prison and post-release. Both prison and adult education policy and funding frameworks are shaped by a discourse of empowerment that promotes self-regulation and internalised control around neoliberal employability and enterprise priorities. Prison radio training was able to grow within these frameworks, while equally representing resistance against such strategies of individualised responsibility. The project differences relate to the ways in which it engages with prisoners, how it treats prisoners, and how it aims to work collaboratively with them to identify strategies to work constructively within the system.

Inglis is influenced by the 1988 work of Michael Collins, who presents a scathing attack on self-directed learning in which he argues that education and training in prisons is essentially 'accommodative' rather than 'transformative'. Through work with prisoners and educators in Canada, he presents 'disturbing insights' into the coercive structures and power relationships that impact on prison education but also shape wider adult education practice (Collins, 1988, p.101). Describing the prison setting in order to contextualise education provision, he shows the 'all-pervasive surveillance' through security checks and the control of movement of prisoners and staff, but also supported through the hierarchical structure and architecture of the prison. He argues that prison staff are subject to more reporting and accountability checks than outside employees and agencies, resulting in a 'watchful and distrustful' environment designed to individuate and control the population, which then 'infiltrates' education provision (Collins, 1988, p.103).

For Collins, education merely becomes an adjunct to the overall apparatus of surveillance, regulation and punishment, part of the strategy to treat, correct and infantilise criminals as delinquents and operating as a deeply embedded normalising technology (Clements 2004, p.171). While presenting a wholly negative account of prison education in the 1980s, Collins provides a useful context for the emergence of more creative and prisoner-focused provision later. Interestingly for this study, while his critique is particularly damning, it recognises a small amount of activity which breaks away from the disciplinary and panoptic model:

> It would certainly be enlightening to find out what qualities drive and sustain those prison educators who do comprehend fully what they are up against and yet manage to resist by creating small, somewhat autonomous sites of civilised discourse in an otherwise hostile environment. (Collins 1988, p.109)

Developing in the following decade, prison radio is representative of such pockets of resistance, while its continued success illustrates the extent to which genuine transformative learning and personal development can be achieved in prison. Both the West Midlands project evaluation and later interviews with key participants suggest that this is based on attitudes towards people, and a respectful, supportive and collaborative approach that is central not only to partnership working, but also to practical teaching endeavours and the media production process.

Project design and delivery

The evaluation report identifies 'people and partnerships' as the key to the success of the radio training project with feedback from the range of stakeholders including prisoners, prison managers, funders and partner organisations, stressing the importance of the personalities and values of those involved in the process, from the earliest stages of development (Wilkinson and Davidson 2008). The project development and negotiation processes were identified as crucial to successful delivery, ensuring that all appropriate staff were involved from the earliest stages of planning (2008, p.18). For instance, the proposal for newly appointed external staff to enter a prison with electronic equipment to deliver a short course is fraught with potential practical and security challenges and successful negotiation of access into each prison is recognised as both an achievement and a learning outcome within the project: 'PRA staff reported that being flexible and open to individual discussions was the biggest learning point they came away from negotiating access with the four prisons involved' (Wilkinson and Davidson 2008, p.19).

The enthusiasm, flexibility and creativity of PRA and prison staff are highlighted throughout the process (Wilkinson and Davidson 2008, p.3), with PRA Project Co-ordinator Jules McCarth, recounting the importance of bringing together the Head of Reducing Reoffending and the HOLS early on, to work out what was needed and think creatively about how it could work. This is particularly demonstrated through the case of HMP Long Lartin, the highest security prison involved in the project. Showing their commitment to the activity, three members of the Senior Management Team visited an earlier training session in another prison to see the project in action and speak with McCarthy at length. Rather than making the process more difficult, the higher security level of the prison was felt to contribute to the setting up of the project: "Everyone wants to try and iron out any potential pitfalls before they happen" (McCarthy in Wilkinson and Davidson 2008, p.18). Through communication, flexibility and negotiation in the earliest stages, the project details and practices were amended and adapted to account for the need for extra security for all involved and the evaluation found that delivery staff successfully 'honed' their negotiating skills at each stage:

'In terms of the overall project the idea was to test things out and test how they worked and we certainly have learnt a lot in terms of just how different each prison is and how they go about things.' (McCarthy in Wilkinson and Davidson 2008, p.18)

The commitment of those involved to finding ways to make a unique and potentially challenging project work can be attributed to an enthusiasm for new and innovative activity. However, the training was not universally accepted and encouraged. The prisons that failed to take up the opportunity were unsurprisingly concerned about the practical challenges of setting up a short-term project within an overstretched and under-resourced prison system (Wilkinson and Davidson 2008). Even within the participating prisons, the additional work involved in moving equipment, and escorting visiting staff and prisoners daily was not always well received by prison officers and managers. The success of the courses is recognised as dependent on the flexibility and creativity of those involved, with reluctant staff gradually witnessing the benefits for prisoners and prison alike.

The course design and delivery mark the major point of difference with traditional, more accommodative learning strategies, based on the principle of treating prisoners as people, with the potential to learn and achieve. The evaluation recognises two critical success factors based on the practical content and positive delivery: the engagement of enthusiastic delivery staff that were committed to motivating learners to fulfil their potential; and a training course that was delivered in a practical and supportive way that learners felt valued as 'equals' and 'not spoken down to' (Wilkinson and Davidson 2008, pp.53–54).

McCarthy's teaching style and attitude towards prisoners are identified as central to the process, able to engage learners through practical and enjoyable activity while remaining focused on the skills development objectives of the wider project. Training was designed to embed basic skills and create opportunities for learners to contemplate future career pathways by working on specific radio production projects in small groups. Group work enhanced spoken communication skills while the time set aside to produce individual journals developed literacy and ICT skills. In addition, project themes involved opportunities for self-reflection around issues of rehabilitation and were presented in ways that were both relevant and engaging for learners, with Wilkinson and Davidson (2008, p.20) citing two examples:

- 'Keeping it Real Behind the Steel', where prisoners discussed the subject of restorative justice; and
- 'ETE, a One-Way Ticket out of HMP', helping prisoners to think about opportunities on release.

During each course, learners produced audio material that was edited and copied to CD, typically consisting of personal statements, news items, group discussion on the realities of prison life, and interviews with prison staff (Wilkinson and Davidson 2008, p.28). Learners actively participated in identifying and defining the chosen topics for discussion with other projects including financial literacy, volunteering opportunities outside prison, and the charity work of rapper Tupac Shakur, a topic which epitomises the trainer's ability to combine learners' interests with discussion on issues of social responsibility. In most cases the audio was then used to help with the prison induction process, explaining the workings of prison life, including interviews with prison departments such as healthcare, gym staff, canteen operators and drug treatment workers (Wilkinson and Davidson 2008, p.28).

The ability to integrate the curriculum with practical activity was seen as a strength by learners, prison staff and partner organisations, with one education provider describing the courses as "Skills by the back door ... They don't feel like they're learning basic skills and soft skills too" (Wilkinson and Davidson 2008, p.35). For learners, the focus on creative programme production provided a stark contrast to previous experiences of traditional 'school-type' lessons, with all describing it as a far more positive learning option (Wilkinson and Davidson 2008, p.49). Creative activities encourage people back into learning, and provide a positive alternative that develops critical thinking skills, leading to further learning. As a reintroduction to education for those with negative previous experiences, engaging the eyes and hands of students inevitably leads to their minds, providing a valuable opportunity to explore individual potential and increase self-esteem: 'Once interested in the arts, students will be more willing to look at more mundane and less attractive educational options, those for instance linked to the basic skills curriculum' (Clements 2004, p.173).

Feedback from both learners and the prison staff directly involved in the delivery of the project highlight McCarthy's approach to teaching and attitude towards the learners as a critical success factor:

> 'The success of this is down to the personality of the people who've delivered this course because if you didn't get somebody who was innovative and exciting and dynamic it could have all gone a very different way.' (Education Provider in Wilkinson and Davidson 2008, p.50)

While individual personalities and attitudes are central to any positive and effective learning strategy, both the project evaluation and McCarthy's later reflection highlight two additional factors that remain fundamental to the success of prison radio: a passion for radio; and treating prisoners as people.

McCarthy's attitude to prisoners is reflected throughout her interview (2012), always referring to 'people' or 'learners' rather than 'prisoners' or 'offenders', and describing the work as 'humbling'. This is best illustrated through the account of her first encounter with prisoners as a BBC Regional news reporter working on a project designed to shed light on the range of criminal justice procedures and processes. Visiting HMP Shrewsbury, she describes the "Dickensian dungeon of a prison" and talks of her shock at meeting with a group of alleged armed robbers:

> 'I think I was expecting McVicar and the Kray Twins ... I was stunned to find they were perfectly ordinary teenage boys and any one of them could have been my teenage sons ... It really got to me because there was ordinariness about these boys that made me realise that prison can happen to anybody's son.' (McCarthy 2012)

The reaction mirrors the values of fellow PRA founders, linked to a realisation that many people in prison are only a set of circumstances, choices and chances away from ourselves. Rather than considering prisoners as demonised villains, prison radio is based on a belief that with the right conditions and opportunities, people can achieve. McCarthy talks of feeling that this was a field in which she could make a difference, of being inspired to volunteer with a local youth group, and of her enthusiasm when the PRA opportunity came up, themes which are both similar to those of colleagues' accounts and connect to the pathways, values and motivations of volunteers and social activists outlined previously.

Discussing her transition from the BBC to teaching in prison, McCarthy expresses her shock at the degree to which people stagnate and demonstrates a continued belief in the transformative potential of education: "you are closed down as a human being". Accounts of the radio courses describe a supportive and non-authoritarian approach to teaching based on a starting point of mutual respect that facilitates a civilised discourse within prison. This was identified as a major strength and, in comparison with previous experiences of school, learner feedback shows they 'felt that they were shown more respect, felt that the radio trainer treated them like adults and equals' (Wilkinson and Davidson 2008, p.49).

The tutor's attitude may have fostered a respectful learning environment, yet the dynamic was equally influenced by the prisoner perceptions and assumptions about her as a media professional from outside the prison. Describing her first meeting with a new group of learners, they were impressed by her BBC background and queried why she would spend the time teaching them. In contrast, McCarthy (2012) felt it was a privilege that they were talking to her: "they wanted to know why we were wasting our time talking to them. You are never wasting your time with somebody". Learners' respect for McCarthy's role as an outside, industry professional was further reflected through feedback on the masterclass element of the project with broadcasters from the BBC, CSV Media and Birmingham City University visiting the prisons to be interviewed by the group in order to share their skills and experiences. Again, the BBC connection is felt to add credibility to the activity, yet for all involved in direct delivery, the PRA's status as an independent and separate entity was identified as a strength, able to bring new people, skills and perspectives into the prison and perceived as outside the mainstream prison apparatus.

The PRA's radio training activity played a pivotal role in determining and shaping this objective, with education recognised as an important element in the formalisation and acceptance of their work from the early stages. The ability to support and work with radio training projects run by existing prison education partners remains pivotal to the success of NPR, engaging prisoners in the production process and ensuring the station remains relevant and interesting for listeners. The West Midlands project marks the beginning of this process, with the PRA able to demonstrate the benefits and potential of prison radio to a range of key stakeholders including prisoners, prisons, education partners and funders. On a prison level, it provided evidence that radio could contribute to reducing reoffending performance targets, while for education providers and funding agencies, the partnership demonstrated the ability to raise qualification levels through new delivery models. For the PRA, the project provided an opportunity to build the relationships and knowledge to work with partners to mainstream radio training in prisons, while the evaluation process helped to build a body of evidence to support the expansion of prison radio and the development of a national service.

Summary

In this and the preceding chapter, I have focused on the relationships and institutional arrangements that were considered as central to the growth of prison radio at a particular time. Examination of the political and institutional contexts of two regional partnership projects served to illustrate the process. Discussion of the role of the BBC in developing the West Midlands prison radio partnership illustrated the formal establishment of the PRA, and an analysis of the prison radio training project demonstrated the development of the organisation's strategic vision. Together, these projects show the importance of people and partnerships in driving the development of prison radio. PRA growth is linked to the governmental restructuring of public services through devolved partnership arrangements based on business innovation and enterprise. Equally, however, the perspectives of the prisoners, practitioners and partners involved show that activity is driven by the passion, commitment and skills of individuals who believe that people in prison deserve a chance and should be treated with empathy and respect.

The PRA's early partnership working in the West Midlands region illustrates the ways in which founders were able to work flexibly and creatively within a shifting environment, shaped by increasing managerialism and performance targets. This demonstrates that the ability to navigate and creatively adapt to complex and shifting prison frameworks is underpinned by the passion, commitment and values of those involved. Discussion of both the regional steering group and training project illustrates the PRA's focus on building positive and constructive relationships with stakeholders. In the following two chapters, attention turns to the challenges involved in developing prison radio further and the ways in which the PRA navigated the process. The challenges presented by negative and unrealistic perceptions about prison radio are outlined before focusing on two prominent examples that emerged through participant accounts. The PRA management of mainstream media coverage in the lead up to the launch of NPR is discussed, followed by the later production and reception of an NPR restorative justice radio documentary.

6

Changing The Prison Narrative: The PRA and News Media

Throughout participant accounts of establishing the PRA and NPR, managing external misconceptions and misrepresentations emerges as a significant discursive theme, one which warrants further investigation in relation to the challenges faced by those trying to enact change within a beleaguered prison system. PRA founders described an acute awareness that negative mainstream media attention could lead to the withdrawal of institutional and political support at a critical time in the process of establishing NPR. Mistrust of mainstream media outlets is mirrored across the criminal justice sector, with scholars and practitioners recognising the simplified and negative portrayal of prison issues as a barrier to innovation and change (Sparks 2001; Di Ronco 2016). As a team of experienced media professionals, PRA founders chose to keep a low profile throughout early development, focusing instead on developing quality radio for a unique target audience and only producing outside media campaigns on their own terms, based on major achievements.

The role of mainstream media in creating and sustaining moral panics around crime and punishment is well documented (Hall et al 2013 [1978]; Howitt 1998, pp.25–27; Jewkes 2015), leading to a mistrust among criminal justice practitioners, scholars and activists (Barak 1988; Di Ronco 2016). This position is addressed in Barak's 'Newsmaking Criminology' theory which calls for criminologists to directly engage with mass media, highlighting the role they can play in creating more realistic representations of the social, political and economic conditions of crime and crime control (Barak 1988, p.566). However, today's dispersed and democratised media landscape provides increased opportunities to both disrupt and create newsmaking processes. This chapter uses the PRA experience to illustrate the ways in which criminal justice practitioners, scholars and activists can bypass simplistic, dramatic mass media representations of prison issues and contribute to the production of alternative discourses, shifting the prison narrative from failure to positive change.

The PRA experience illustrates the problematic relationship between mainstream media and prison practice. Its subsequent response demonstrates the potential to reclaim media power through producing more realistic and nuanced representations of prisons and prisoners. First, the PRA position is used to examine the interplay between media and public opinion, and the resulting impact on criminal justice policy and practice. The issues are then explored more fully through the analysis of three contemporary newspaper stories which PRA founders identify as impacting on the organisation's early approach to managing outside media attention. The examples from the *Guardian*, the *Daily Mail*, and *The Sun* newspapers illustrate the co-dependent relationship between mass media coverage, populist politics and perceived public opinion when it comes to the divisive, emotive and increasingly political issue of crime and punishment. This is followed by analysis of a later, critically acclaimed PRA radio documentary which marks a turning point in the acceptance of prison radio beyond the criminal justice sphere.

Prison and news media

Prison theorists acknowledge an overall shift towards populist criminal justice policy in late modernity, with punitive attitudes gaining increased influence in the political domain (Brownlee 1998; Garland 2001; Sim 2009; Wacquant 2009). News media play a central role in the process, functioning as a crucial mediating link between the public and policy makers (Hall et al 2013 [1978]). The role of the media in influencing public opinion and policy has been firmly established by scholars, yet where the power and agency lies in the process remains widely argued and highly contentious (Mason 2007, p.491). Sim describes a 'coincidence of interests' (2009) between mainstream media and politicians when addressing crime and solutions, while others present a co-dependent, symbiotic relationship between the two, supporting and feeding off each other in a cycle of retributionist rhetoric (Mason 2006; Wacquant 2010; Cheliotis 2010). However, as Bottoms' 'populist punitiveness' theory shows, policy is not based on a straightforward reaction to the needs of the people, but on the manipulation of perceived public opinion in order to serve political interests, conveying the notion of 'politicians tapping into, and using for their own purposes, what they believe to be the public's generally punitive stance' (Bottoms 1995, p.40).

The extent to which the public is naturally punitive is questionable; instead, the process is part of a wider complex through which definitive discourses around political and social issues are constructed as a means of control (Sim 2009). Sim describes a self-reinforcing relationship between state officials and the media with crime and punishment discourses increasingly characterised by the soundbites and tabloidisation of populist politics (2009, p.72). Rather than presenting a total synchronicity between the media and politicians, he argues that they are 'yoked in a cycle of mutually reproducing, narrowly defined discourses' around law and order (Sim 2009, p.73).

Where the vast majority of the general public have little or no direct experience of the criminal justice system, mediated representations of prisons play a critical role in informing opinion and policy. Yet cultural resources around crime and prison are limited, and understanding and reactions are predominately informed by oversimplified and overdramatic mass media representations (Green 2009, p.524). Highlighting an increasingly punitive discourse in relation to criminal justice issues, Green argues that there is rarely a 'hydraulic relationship' between public attitudes and policy, outlining a range of influencing factors which impact on each other (2009, p.520). Attitudes are linked to anger, outrage, concern and fear about a rise in crime, all factors that implicate media content. He stops short of suggesting that media creates and shapes public attitudes and opinions, arguing instead that, within a new, diverged mediascape, mass media merely fortifies and sustains already held beliefs (Green 2009, p.519).

However, as mainstream media remains the primary means through which prison is made visible to the public, responsibility for creating punitive attitudes should not be underestimated. As Cheliotis argues, the mediated visibility of the prison serves to 'naturalise, moralise and perpetuate the physical marginalisation of convict populations' (2010, p.170). He attacks mass media for: overstating the problem of crime; placing blame on marginalised groups; criticising the prison administration for laxity; and issuing urgent calls for stricter imprisonment and increased community and individual responsibility for crime. Rather than inform debate, the effect is to feed moral panics about safety and create a criminal enemy while simultaneously protecting the power of corporations (Cheliotis 2010).

In these terms, media representations of prison are overtly political, supporting punitive government policy and justifying the prison expansionist agenda. As Mason argues, media provide the conditions of support for the penal system through the over-reporting of violent and sexual crime:

> The media construct the prison as the essential cornerstone of criminal justice... through its discourses around dangerousness and fear, the perceived 'soft touch' liberalism of prison regimes and increases in prisoners' rights. At the same time, media representations shroud the reality of prison as an instrument of pain delivery and ignore

> the collateral damage to prisoners' families. (Mason 2006, p.253)

Through the analysis of a snapshot of prison stories in British newspapers, Mason demonstrates that the discourse of the prisoner dehumanises the prison experience, subverting any real debate about alternatives. The public is led to believe that prisons are full of violent criminals living in luxury at the taxpayers' expense while left un-informed about the harsh realities of prison life (Mason, 2006, p.263). Where media depict prison as an institution full of murderers, rapists and paedophiles, the realities of prison life go largely un-noticed in the public domain, including dramatic increases in suicide and self-harm and the rising number of women and children incarcerated (2006, p.251). Instead of cultivating communitarian solutions towards the problems of crime, media play on public fears and overstate the danger of criminal victimisation, thereby targeting already marginalised groups (Cheliotis 2010).

These arguments illustrate the challenges faced by the criminal justice sector and demonstrate the significance of prison media, both in terms of facilitating realistic and constructive representations of prisoners and in supporting the work of those involved in managing and instigating change within an overstretched and unworkable prison system. Sparks (2001, p.6) acknowledges 'a deep-rooted frustration and anger' towards the media among criminal justice researchers and practitioners. He questions whether there is in fact a 'malign intent' to inflame public passions and play on fears, highlighting an endless concentration on bad news about crime that reduces innovative research findings and progressive initiatives to soundbites (Sparks 2001, p.6). Solomon (2005) too observes a disdain, even 'pure venom' on occasion, towards the media throughout the criminal justice sector, calling for a change in approach for getting the message across about the complexities of crime.

Reputational risk

During the development of NPR, the founders talk of being "desperately media-shy", recognising the need to keep a low profile and only turning to the media when they had something specific to shout about (Maguire 2012). "Something happening" or "something going wrong" is discussed as the greatest risk to the project, linked to attracting attention and negative publicity for both themselves and prison partners:

> 'The biggest threat to prison radio is ... something happening in a prison radio studio ... the wrong person going on air, the wrong person saying something on air, something going on air that somehow gets leaked out to a newspaper, and there's a headline in a newspaper about prison radio that scares the politicians and they close down the project.' (Maguire 2012)

In the 18 months leading up to the launch of NPR, three media incidents are identified by founders as impacting on the development of the project, all of which illustrate the problematic relationship between media, policy and practice. The first example, in the *Daily Mail* newspaper, relates to a separate project, yet the coverage and repercussions typify the risks of negative publicity for progressive prison initiatives. 'The *Daily Mail* factor' emerges as an ongoing and significant discursive theme throughout the accounts of NPR founders, becoming symbolic of the challenges they faced and representing the antithesis of what they were trying to achieve. PRA co-founder and Chair, Roma Hooper, talks of applying the '*Daily Mail* test' to early prison radio, asking what a typical reader would think of content or activity, continually mindful of how the project could be perceived and criticised by the punitive, retributionist right. The *Daily Mail* newspaper purports to be the voice of middle England, with the UK's second highest average daily circulation of almost 3.5 million (Newsworks 2016a), second only to the News Corp tabloid, *The Sun*. Originally designed as a middle-market newspaper for the lower middle classes, positioned between the sensationalist and entertainment-based tabloids and the high-end journalism of the broadsheets, it has traditionally supported the Conservative Party and epitomises populist, punitive attitudes about prison and prisoners. The '*Daily Mail* factor' is used repeatedly by PRA founders to describe the process of managing the risks of negative publicity, signifying the newspaper's influence on informing public opinion and impacting on prison practice.

Prison radio is representative of the range of innovative creative projects developing and operating in prisons, designed to engage prisoners in constructive activity, self-reflection and personal change. Music, drama, singing, cooking or art projects are recognised on an institutional level and are more recently gaining a public profile through documentary and reality television programmes. Yet activities are usually stand-alone, driven by volunteers, and surviving from day to day subject to the proclivities of short-term funding opportunities. *The Comedy School* runs stand-up comedy workshops in prisons to help people become more articulate, to build confidence, to interact with other prisoners, and develop their speaking and listening skills. On 22 November 2008, the project featured in the *Daily Mail* after a convicted Al Qaeda terrorist took part in a class at HMP Whitemoor Maximum Security Prison (McDermott 2008). As a result, funding was withdrawn, the course was cancelled, and staff were immediately removed from the prison, demonstrating the speed and severity of reactions to mass media outrage.

The *Daily Mail* story builds on the fear of terrorism, opening with details of the prisoner and his offence before outlining the Justice Secretary, Jack Straw's, reaction to the news, immediately halting the workshop and branding the scheme "totally unacceptable" (McDermott 2008). Here, perceived public outrage becomes Straw's own, placing responsibility for such mistakes at the feet of prison governors and warning them to "take account of the public acceptability test" when approving courses (Straw, in McDermott 2008). The public acceptability angle and prominence of Straw's response within the story is indicative of governmental efforts to extend public responsibility and accountability in crime and criminal justice issues. However, the incident equally illustrates the contradictions of social authoritarianism, at once facilitating and supporting education and rehabilitation priorities within prison while engaging in tough punitive rhetoric and knee-jerk reactions to negative press on the outside.

Right-wing tabloid newspaper, *The Sun*, broke the story on 21 November 2008 with a more emotive piece describing the 'evil' terrorist learning alongside 'murderers and rapists', representing the sensationalised, over-dramatic portrayal of prisoners. The issue was picked up by the *Telegraph* and the *Guardian* on the same day carrying similar, yet smaller, and less prominent coverage. However, the *Guardian* story was followed up with an editorial piece by Mark Fisher (2008) in defence of *The Comedy School*. For Fisher, the closure of the project is indicative not only of the government's punitive stance but an ongoing obsession with how it is perceived by the press. Outlining his own experience of visiting a playwriting workshop at a Young Offenders Institution, he echoes similar responses to prison radio, citing the governor's support for creative projects, 'he believes participation in the arts triggers behavioural change among inmates and affects the mood of a whole establishment' (Fisher 2008). As Fisher highlights, these are the criteria on which rehabilitation programmes should be based rather than Straw's vague declaration of 'appropriate' (McDermott 2008).

Jack Straw plays a central role in the PRA story by approving NPR while heading the newly formed Ministry of Justice in 2007. Paradoxically, however, his reputation for being notoriously punitive in reaction to perceived popular opinion is illustrated through his reaction to *The Comedy School* episode. His response in the *Daily Mail* emphasises the role of the responsible taxpayer community working in partnership with the government to shape solutions and combat the effects of crime, "There is a crucial test: can the recreational, social and educational classes paid for out of taxpayers' money (or otherwise) be justified to the community?" (Straw, in McDermott 2008). Similarly, PRA founders recognise the need to continually demonstrate the benefits of prison radio. Yet rather than changing minds of those large sections of the general public who remain largely misinformed by mainstream commercial media, they focus instead on the opinions of stakeholders and partners within the prison community and wider criminal justice system.

PRA founders all talk of the dangers of being 'tricked' and 'tripped up' by the press on the lookout for potential scandal (Tilley, Hooper, Robinson and McDowell 2012) and the endless quest for 'bite-sized chunks' of information (Sim 2009, p.73). PRA Trustee and former HM Chief Inspector of Probation, Paul McDowell, was governor of HMP Brixton at the time, and a key driver behind the establishment of the national service. He recalls an early brush with outside media coverage following the launch of flagship station, Electric Radio Brixton. The incident illustrates the sensationalist tendencies of the press in relation to prison issues, while equally implicating the left wing press in the process. McDowell attended the Radio Festival in Nottingham in June 2009. At the broadcast industry event he was interviewed on air by entertainments-based radio and television presenter, Richard Bacon. Having raised the point that many people would think that prisoners should not be provided with enjoyable activities like radio, Bacon asked "do you not think that this is a *Daily Mail* story waiting to happen?" McDowell successfully managed to avoid the question before being asked a third time in a different way and "falling into the trap" (2012), with a tweet from an audience member resulting in the *Guardian* headline: 'Brixton prison radio 'a *Daily Mail* story waiting to happen', says governor' (Plunkett 2009).

For McDowell (2012), the incident perfectly illustrates the reputational risks that prison radio represents in the public domain, resulting in simplified, and negative representations of complex issues. Even when reported in a traditionally left-leaning, quality broadsheet such as the *Guardian*, prison radio is reduced to tabloid tactics that perpetuate the discourses of dangerousness and cost that dominate the prison debate. Electric Radio Brixton is described as 'Sony award-winning', yet the first descriptor used is 'taxpayer-funded', pandering to the populist view of prison as ineffectual, lax and draining the public purse. Setting the tone for the story, it goes on to quote McDowell on the need to bar certain inmates from the airwaves 'to protect the project from attack from the *Daily Mail*' (Plunkett 2009).

The opening sentences illustrate the prevalent themes throughout the reporting of prison issues, highlighting perceived public concerns over cost, and moderate treatment of prisoners, as well as a fascination with high-profile prisoners and potential for scandal. The *Daily Mail* factor is presented as the driving force behind recruitment rather than any educational strategy, with the rehabilitory aims of the project relegated to the final third of the story. Not only does the coverage highlight the potential for something to go wrong but exaggerates the risks, suggesting the inevitability of scandal:

> 'I am a prison governor and half of my life is spent managing the politics of prisoners. One of the things I am not going to do is put Ian Huntley on a radio station to deliver a programme every week. That is opening us up [to attack] and if we get criticised for that then we might end up losing the whole thing.' (McDowell, in Plunkett 2009)

As an early example of mainstream media coverage of prison radio, the story in the *Guardian* illustrates tabloid tendencies around prison issues based on perceived punitive public attitudes, even outside the right wing tabloids. Yet the reader comments below the online version of the story show an overwhelming support for creative rehabilitory measures in prison, and express concern about the dangers of a *Daily Mail* mentality, indicating a continued commitment to issues of social justice among readers: "Totally happy for my taxes to go towards creative rehabilitative activities for prisoners" (M0ngrel, 30 June 2009 3:53pm, The Guardian Online).

Throughout their accounts, PRA founders identified the risk that negative tabloid coverage at the beginning of the project could lead to the immediate cancellation of radio training, production and broadcasting in prisons. Yet while the '*Daily Mail* factor' features repeatedly, the most prominent example mentioned is a front page story in *The Sun* on 20 January 2009. Owned by Rupert Murdoch's News Corp, *The Sun* remains the biggest selling newspaper in the UK with an average daily print readership of over 4 million (Newsworks 2016b). While the print media industry is under considerable threat from the proliferation of digital platforms, the continued popularity of *The Sun* demonstrates its status and influence on the UK media landscape, purporting to be the voice of the skilled working classes and loudly supporting Conservative Party values and policies. The primary aim of the newspaper is entertainment, focusing on television and celebrity news together with salacious, titillating drama and scandal.

Hooper describes the tabloid tactic of putting flyers on windscreens in prison car parks to hunt for stories, highlighting the status of prisons as a source of potentially controversial, emotive and political content. After a Prison Service Order announcing the development of NPR had been issued, a disgruntled prison officer is said to have called *The Sun* (Hooper 2012), resulting in a front page story with a page seven spread. The story does not name the PRA at any point and only lasted for one day, with minimal overall impact on the development of the project. However, the incident epitomises the coverage that the PRA was so keen to avoid, and the challenges that mainstream media represent within the criminal justice sector:

> 'So even before we got going with broadcasting the service, one of the tabloids wanted to shut us down, and that was even before we started the project. From that day we decided to take a very low press profile, because we knew that a nervous minister could switch us off if it created bad press.' (Tilley 2012)

Prison radio covers one third of the front page of *The Sun* on 20 January 2009 with the headlines 'Prisons Exclusive' and 'CON AIR' combining to create a sense of drama and danger through reference to the Hollywood action film of the same name. The subheading, 'Lags' Radio Station to Cost Public £2m' repeats the economic concerns noted in previous examples of prison news coverage while invoking the prisoner as both lazy and expensive. The term 'lags' is of particular significance, used as the main descriptor for prisoners throughout the story, appearing twice on the front page and twice again on page seven. Rather than the young street thug most usually invoked by politicians, or the gangster criminal favoured in dramatic portrayals of prison, 'lag' refers to old, long term, entrenched criminals in the style of comedy character Norman Stanley Fletcher from 1970s British television sitcom, Porridge. In a typically tabloid play on words, the term also suggests failure, slackness and slowing others down, presenting prisoners as failing to achieve economic success as well as being financially draining for the general public. Through focus on the habitual career criminal, prisoners are presented as beyond the reach of rehabilitation initiatives, a move which simultaneously recognises and challenges the rehabilitory aims of prison radio. Mason too notes its use as a peculiarly tabloid device, noting an example in the *Daily Star* where the construction of prisoners as 'lags' 'evokes a cosy, comic notion of knockabout farce' (Mason 2006, p.259) that reinforces the view of prison as a soft option and obscures the issues of prison overcrowding and under-funding.

The Sun coverage of prison radio is similarly framed in comic terms, presenting the idea as 'ridiculous' (Kay 2009). The introductory text on the front page expresses outrage and incredulity about the potential cost, 'PAMPERED lags are to get their OWN radio station' (Kay 2009) while in the full story on page seven, comic language and imagery feature more heavily. The chief reporter writes that, 'Jail plans to blow millions on a new radio station beaming pop and chat to cells nationwide sparked fury' (Kay 2009, p.7). The text is accompanied by a picture of 1990s fictional comedy DJ characters 'Smashy and Nicey' with Jack Straw's face superimposed as Nicey. Straw is attacked as responsible for funding an 'inappropriate' initiative and ridiculed through portrayal as a tacky, comical radio presenter talking nonsense. The story is used as a political attack, with responsibility placed firmly in the hands of 'Jack Straw', 'officials', and the 'Prison Service' with the PRA only referred to once, as 'a charity': 'The Prison Service, which came up with the idea claimed the £2 million to start the station up would come out of existing budgets and a charity would chip in with the running costs' (Kay 2009, p.7).

The notional figure of '£2 million' is repeated four times throughout the story, reinforcing economic fear and attributing blame on the government for irresponsible and profligate spending of taxpayers' money. Shadow Justice Minister Edward Garnier provides the main response, 'blasting' the cost to taxpayers and describing a national prison radio service as a 'cock-eyed waste' (Kay 2009). His is the main voice throughout the story, quoted in informal and friendly tones, representing the voice of the people, while the faceless officials of the Prison Service are presented as formal and detached.

The Prison Service is called on to defend the idea 'amid outrage', claiming 'cuts meant inmates spent more time in their cell'. Yet while the underlying issue of prison funding is acknowledged, it is given more prominence through Garnier's response, used as a political manoeuvre in order to accuse the government of presiding over 'the worst prison overcrowding in the history of the Prison Service' (Kay 2009). Garnier's response takes precedence over the practical aims of the project. While the informative and educational focus is mentioned, it directly follows the subheading 'Ridiculous', and a statement that the station would carry 'messages and educational programmes' is set in quotation marks in sneering tones and presented as the words of a nameless 'official'.

The idea of a national prison radio service is set in comic tones with prisoners repeatedly referred to as 'pampered', living a luxurious life 'lying on their beds listening to Jack Straw twittering at them over the radio' (Kay 2009). The description not only reinforces the notion of the 'lazy' prisoner but ridicules Straw as ineffectual and unimportant, further validating the comments of the Conservative opposition as the voice of the hard-working people. Through a comic narrative set in tones of outrage and incredulity, the story reconstructs the issues of prison funding and prisoner rehabilitation as governmental and Prison Service failures.

The comedic representation of prison radio is epitomised on page seven through a creative programme schedule parody. 'TODAY ON RADIO CON' repeats the Con Air reference on the front page, playing on 'con' both as shorthand for convict while also implying conning the public out of money, inferring that both politicians and prisoners are con artists who will cheat good people out of their hard-earned money. A mock rundown of the broadcast day then features programme titles and announcers which play on the theme of dangerousness, 'presented' by high profile violent criminals including a serial killer, a serial rapist, a mother convicted of kidnapping her own daughter, and Islamic fundamentalist Abu Hamza.

Hooper (2012) describes *The Sun* coverage of prison radio as "diabolical". Prisoners are presented as 'pampered lags', prisons as ineffectual, and radio as a waste of taxpayers' money. Not only does the story reinforce the notion of prison as a soft option but plays on misconceptions about radio as solely music-based entertainment, obscuring the information and education potential. While the story represents a direct and potentially difficult challenge to the work of the PRA, prison radio is only featured for one day, quickly overshadowed by the inauguration of Barack Obama as US president. The minor impact on NPR development can be attributed to the relatively short time the project spent in the spotlight combined with the degree of government support and senior level endorsement garnered by that stage.

The PRA media strategy

The PRA celebrated ten years of operations in 2016. During this time, the organisation has gained credibility within the criminal justice, broadcasting and non-profit sectors, winning numerous industry awards for the quality of its work and establishing radio as an integral feature in prisons in England and Wales. The successful development can in part be attributed to the organisation's tight control over media coverage and careful management of outside perceptions of its activities and achievements. As prison radio has become more established, negative coverage poses less of a direct risk, yet there is still a reticence about engaging with mainstream media outlets. For the Chief Executive, Maguire, the challenges may be different, but the reasoning remains the same. The PRA exists to represent prisoners, not to convince the public about the benefits of prison radio (Maguire 2016).

The Prison Service is 'incredibly media-shy', and the organisation has focused on developing a positive working relationship with the Ministry of Justice press office. Responding to unsolicited media enquiries and ensuring press office clearance can be a lengthy process, seen as detracting from the core aims. Instead, as a media organisation, the PRA is able to develop its own media campaigns, based on major developments and achievements. The *Daily Mail* factor demonstrates the perceptions and attitudes that prison radio seeks to counteract, informing and shaping the PRA's media strategy. To illustrate the approach, Maguire gives the example of managing the media coverage of the PRA's nominations for the 2009 Sony Radio Academy Awards:

'We were the biggest story of the Sony's that year. People hadn't really heard of prison radio before within the radio industry, and for us to win two Golds and two Bronzes at the Sony's, it was just an incredible thing.' (Maguire 2012)

In the run up to the awards, they were aware that the nominations could lead to media interest and made the decision to carefully manage the process by contacting specific journalists they felt would understand and represent prison radio in an intelligent and appropriate way: *Guardian* columnist Zoe Williams; former BBC media correspondent Torin Douglas; and *The Times* media editor, Dan Sabbagh, later to become news editor at the *Guardian*. Maguire (2012) talks of "inviting" selected journalists to write about the work of the PRA, and "allowing them access", indicating the importance of overseeing the process and the need to reclaim control from potentially unsupportive media.

In addition to select interviews, a press pack was compiled for the website. Maguire stresses the importance of acquiring Ministry of Justice clearance for the press pack, which included a media release on the activities and achievements to date. This was accompanied by the audio that had been nominated for awards and been cleared for broadcast externally. Maguire (2012) then outlines the strategy of withdrawing from media contact completely, "we pulled up the drawbridge" and the PRA team put 'out of office' messages on telephones and emails saying they were not available for comment and referring press enquiries to the website.

From there, Maguire describes the BBC, *Guardian* and *Times* coverage as "going wild", and attracting attention worldwide including stories by the Australian Broadcasting Corporation and *Forbes Magazine* in the United States (2009). Through the awards, the PRA became a huge national and international story, while the media strategy of limiting coverage to three carefully selected features and a one press release ensured that all articles contained the same positive message: "They couldn't misquote anybody, they couldn't twist it, they simply took the message that we put out there and reiterated it across the globe" (Maguire 2012).

For Maguire, the success of the PRA media strategy was the focus on radio. Rather than commentary based on criminal justice, home affairs or social issues, PRA control of the process ensured that prison radio remained a story about radio rather than a story about prison (Maguire 2012). Coverage that focuses on the radio activity and content highlights the project potential and is less likely to be drawn into political wrangling around the perceived successes and failures of the prison system.

Summary

This chapter has analysed three UK newspaper stories published in the 18 months leading up to the launch of the world's first national prison radio service. The coverage of *The Comedy School* in the *Daily Mail* demonstrates the speed and severity of governmental and institutional reactions to bad publicity; the Electric Radio Brixton headline in the *Guardian* illustrates the quest for sensationalist, scandalous sound-bites; and the feature in *The Sun* provides a clear example of the ways in which prison news is used to further political agendas. Combined, the stories typify news media prison discourse, and illustrate a widespread caution and mistrust of news media among criminal justice researchers, practitioners and activists.

As shown here, media discourse and political process are interdependent, particularly in relation to crime and punishment (Sparks 2001). News media plays a central role in justifying and legitimising increasingly coercive forms of social control (Hall et al 2013 [1978]). Through exaggerating and extending the effects of crime, media create moral panics which contribute to public punitiveness and result in greater punishments, while simultaneously precluding any rational debate on alternatives to the prison solution (Cheliotis 2010, p.170). Wacquant describes the process effectively, depicting a form of 'civic theatre' through which politicians dramatise moral norms as means of political manipulation in order to achieve the expansion of the prison state (2010, p.206).

However, as Solomon argues, it is naive to expect newspapers and broadcasters to be responsible conduits of information (2005, p.37). Where media institutions are driven by the need to sell products, news values will inevitably prioritise the dramatic and sensational. Instead, responsibility lies with the criminal justice sector to develop more effective and sophisticated communications strategies. Di Ronco (2016) highlights the role newsmaking criminologists can play through engaging constructively with news media, arguing that they are able to connect issues such as anti-social behaviour to wider and deeper issues of justice and social control, actively changing the frames of reference for discussing crime and punishment.

The PRA experience indicates a separate and complementary approach through which criminal justice scholars, practitioners and activists can reclaim media power. Rather than directly challenging negative and simplistic media representations, the PRA actively avoids news media attention, focusing instead on creating radio that reflects the interests, needs and concerns of the prison community. The PRA experience and strategy for managing outside media attention shows new approaches for criminal justice reformers, supporting Sparks' position 'that more hopeful, constructive and oppositional stories can be told if we can develop the skill and cunning needed to tell them better' (2001, p.7). Through increasing information, communication, and representing the hidden human voices of prison life, prison radio begins to reframe the dominant narrative from one of punishment and retribution to a focus on rehabilitation and positive change.

7

Restorative Justice In Action: The *Face to Face* Documentary

In 2011, *Victim Support* commissioned the PRA to produce a radio documentary that gave three victims of violent crime the opportunity to explain the impact of these crimes to a group of prisoners. *Face to Face* was first broadcast on National Prison Radio on 23 March 2012, and such was the impact that BBC Radio 4 made the rare move of re-broadcasting the programme. For producing a ground-breaking example of restorative justice in action, the PRA and *Victim Support* were named 'Charity Partnership of the Year' at the Third Sector Excellence Awards, and the hour-long documentary won the prestigious 'Gold Sony Radio Academy Award', with the judges describing it as "True 'stop what you're doing' radio. It was a programme that had made a difference to all who had participated in it ... and the judges felt privileged to have heard it" (PRA 2017a).

For those involved, the event marked a significant turning point for the PRA, representing the wider acceptance and legitimacy of prison radio outside the criminal justice field. As both Maguire and Hooper indicate, the key factor is the restorative justice focus. Through bringing the victim's voice into the equation, prison radio no longer risks being perceived as focused solely on the rights of 'undeserving' prisoners but also becomes a platform for victims' expression.

In this chapter, I focus on the context, content and effects of the *Face to Face* programme in furthering the development of the PRA and argue that the case demonstrates the potential of prison radio to promote, facilitate and inform restorative justice practice. First, I examine the restorative justice theme within the contemporary political context before turning to the programme itself, the wider reception and its impact and significance for the PRA. Through discussion of the increasingly victim-centred reporting of crime within mainstream media, I show that prison radio not only provides a voice for prisoners, but is able to empower victims of crime. Both mainstream media and criminal justice policy continue to marginalise those affected by crime, providing limited opportunities for expression of a range of views and largely reducing victims to a homogenous, vulnerable group. In contrast, prison radio facilitates a constructive and respectful discourse which promotes greater understanding between perpetrators and victims of crime, thereby contributing to a process of reconciliation and rehabilitation.

Restorative justice

The concept of restorative justice is based on principles of community responsibility and reconciliation. Focusing on the needs of both the victim and the offender, it not only recognises the need for restitution, but the role the community can play in helping offenders to avoid further criminal situations. Over the past two decades, restorative justice has been adopted and adapted as a progressive solution to the problems of crime, becoming a central theme of UK criminal justice reform, framing new approaches to working with young offenders in particular. On one level, restorative justice represents cooperative, communal and humanitarian solutions to the problems of social exclusion, based on the aim of reconnecting and reconciling offenders with victims, families and communities. Yet government support of such approaches equally points to the adaptation of restorative justice as a neoliberal technology of responsibilisation, framed by a victim-centred discourse. As Patricia Gray (2005) asserts, emerging restorative justice frameworks for the governance of youth crime under New Labour demonstrated a shift in emphasis from 'social justice' to 'moral discipline'. Within this context, the PRA plays an important role in maintaining a balance between victim and prisoner rights, facilitating a dialogue based in empowerment and reconciliation rather than regulation and control.

Summing up the essence of restorative justice, Dennis Sullivan and Larry Tifft refer to the ways that members of the Navajo Nation explain the reasons behind people harming others, describing them as 'acting like they have no family' (2008, p.1). In these terms, the offending person is seen as so disconnected and disengaged from others that the actions are no longer based in personal foundations. Historically, Navajo remedies for such situations focus on the act of healing and call on the families of both parties to help perpetrators to connect or reconnect to the community in a process of 'peacemaking'. Sullivan and Tifft (2008) refer to the Navajo peacemaking process as the quintessential form of restorative justice, involving the whole community in restoring harmony, based on meeting the needs of all concerned.

Such principles form the basis of healing following large-scale collective human rights violations, including the reconciliation process in post-genocide Rwanda and post-apartheid South Africa, and the Australian response to the Stolen Generation of Aboriginal children (Strang and Braithwaite 2001, p.11). The process is broadly based on seeking to reach an agreement, where the needs of those harmed are 'taken into account to the fullest extent possible' (Sullivan and Tifft 2008, p.1). Within such situations, while victim rights are paramount, responsibility for making things right, and to varying extents for the harm itself, falls on the whole community, whether directly, indirectly, actively or passively. The distinctiveness of restorative justice is based on its role as a healing process that involves wider support from families and communities which then engenders greater conflict resolution skills and empowers the community as a whole (Sullivan and Tifft 2008, p.3).

These approaches are based on long-held indigenous customs that aim to meet the needs of all involved in a 'harm situation', 'they know that, if a wrong is not righted in ways that take into account the needs of those who have been affected, the community will eat away at itself' (Sullivan and Tifft 2008, p.2). At the heart of the process is the ability to 'talk things out' to restore harmony (Sullivan and Tifft 2008, p.2). As shown in previous chapters, radio facilitates such conversations within the prison setting, yet the involvement of those whose lives have been affected by crime extends the discussion into the wider community, with the potential to increase information and understanding.

Throughout their accounts, PRA practitioners refer to a largely unrealised potential of existing radio formats to engage audiences in driving content. For Andrew Wilkie, founding Electric Radio Brixton Station Manager and current PRA Director of Radio and Operations, radio performs a crucial community development function within prisons, giving the audience something they can feel proud of:

> 'Building a community is about understanding that there are constructive ways of being, of acting, of interacting with each other. That's what a healthy community does, it interacts and mutually supports each other. That's what media is about in any community, it's about facilitating that interaction, that debate.' (Wilkie 2012)

The wider philosophy of restorative justice becomes a powerful means of community empowerment and democratic participation in ways which mirror that of alternative, non-mainstream radio, indicating a natural merging of both. Where both aim to restore the means of communication and decision making to communities, both equally challenge state power and remain open to governmental and commercial manipulation.

The idea for the *Face to Face* programme came after a prisoner suggested to the PRA that it could improve a show it was making by including the victim's voice. Recognising that it was a good idea, and realising the need for specialist skills, the PRA approached *Victim Support* for help. The charity ended up playing a crucial role in the programme by advising the PRA production team on the issues faced by victims of crime and by ensuring that contributors were chosen appropriately and were supported throughout the recording process. It was an innovative partnership approach which won the 2012 Third Sector Excellence Award, with one of the judges commenting that 'It was a powerful and creative way to deliver on both parties' complementary objectives' (Third Sector 2012).

Based firmly in the non-profit sector, the programme rejects the more retributionist discourse of many mainstream government initiatives, reclaiming the healing principles of restorative justice through equal focus on the needs of both victims and prisoners. While aimed at encouraging prisoners to take responsibility for their actions, choices and decisions, the language and structure of the programme highlight the importance of mutual respect, reframing both victims and prisoners as people, with their own individual stories and perspectives. A governmental shift towards restorative options can be seen as a move towards more humanitarian and community focused solutions to crime, yet initiatives can only thrive when initiated and developed outside state control. While produced within prison, the *Face to Face* programme demonstrates the effectiveness of restorative practice that stems from civil society, as well as the potential of non-mainstream media for promoting and facilitating discussion on prison alternatives.

In contrast to a punitive discourse of 'accountability' and 'responsibility', the joint approach recognises the rehabilitative and restorative priorities of many victims of crime. In an interview for The Restorative Justice Council about the *Face to Face* programme, *Victim Support* Chief Executive Javed Khan highlights the dual benefits of helping victims move forward and preventing criminals from offending again:

> Restorative justice is a way for offenders to make amends and many victims find that it helps the mental scars of the crime to fade away. Victims constantly tell us that one of their key priorities is making sure that offenders don't go on to commit the same crime again and create more victims. Research has found that reoffending among offenders who took part in restorative justice went down by up to 27 percent. (Restorative Justice Council 2012)

The development, production and reception of the programme is based on prisoner rehabilitation and the prevention of crime, building on the potential of individual victims to change the attitudes of prisoners by helping them to recognise the personal effects of crime within a constructive and supportive environment. Victim agency is central to the process, empowering those who have been affected by crime to actively participate in tackling the issues of crime. The *Face to Face* programme provides an opportunity for victims to tell their stories and promote understanding, not only through the recording but through sharing with the wider prison community. Through a radio documentary that focuses on their individual stories, perspectives and reactions, both victims and prisoners are reconstructed as 'people' rather than narrowly defined media constructs.

As Vicky De Mesmaecker argues, the media tendency to focus on the victim alone is a major barrier to the expansion of restorative justice values and practice (2010, p.250). The victim perspective has shifted to centre stage in media coverage of crime over recent decades, a move which Chris Greer describes as one of the most significant qualitative changes in media representations of crime and control since the Second World War: 'victims have taken on an unprecedented significance in media and criminal justice discourses, in the development of crime policy, and in the popular imagination' (Greer 2007, p.21).

Reporting of crime and punishment may have become increasingly victim-centred and generally sympathetic, yet coverage has also been described as 'simplistic, disrespectful, stereotyping and scapegoating' (De Mesmaecker 2010, p.250). Where news reporting of crime is selective and unrepresentative, reporting of crime victims is equally limited, based on representations of those who can be portrayed as the 'ideal victim' (Greer 2007, p.21). Rather than relating to the crime itself, the victim status is afforded to those deemed to be 'worthy' of sympathy, perpetuating the stereotypical construct of a helpless, vulnerable, innocent group (Greer 2007, p.22).

In defining the concept, Nils Christie connects the 'ideal victim' to cultural values and the degree of societal sympathy generated. To illustrate this, he describes 'the little old lady on her way home at midday after caring for her sick sister, hit on the head by a big man who grabs her purse and uses the money to buy drugs' (Christie 1986). In contrast, a drunk young man injured in a bar fight is far from the ideal, with varying levels of sympathy based on the extent of his injuries as well as other contributory factors including age and social status. The legitimacy of victim status is connected to the degree of power, visibility and respect that the person holds in society (Christie 1986). Responsibility and culpability can also be added to the equation, an argument most often invoked in the case of sexual offences against women. As Christie highlights, most real victims and real offenders are ordinary people, rather than culturally constructed 'ideals' and greater understanding of each can only be achieved through increased representation and communication.

Face to Face

Over one hour, the *Face to Face* radio documentary brings together three victims of violent crime with three prisoners serving sentences for similar crimes. The result is a powerful and emotional portrayal of the personal impact of crime, not only in terms of the individuals involved but for the families and loved ones. The programme gained attention outside the prison system, yet is made for a prison target audience with prisoner voices playing a prominent role throughout. Presented by a prisoner, the introduction includes information on seeking support if listeners are affected by any of the content:

> If you are upset by anything you hear in this programme, there are people who can help – speak to a Listener, call a Samaritan, or find someone you can trust and talk to them. (NPR 2012)

The statement is repeated four times, at regular intervals, acknowledging that prisoners too can suffer the psychological and physical effects of crime and are often likely to be emotionally vulnerable. The opening segment foregrounds the prisoner voice and experience, introducing 'Karl, Liam and Adrian' all currently serving sentences at HMP Brixton. With stories that the majority of the prison audience would relate to, they summarise their backgrounds including repeated prison terms from an early age, with offences and sentences escalating each time. Accounts then shift to all three men reflecting on their backgrounds, describing growing up with crime as a 'way of life' characterised by violence and poverty. Liam reflects on his childhood in a traveller community, describing a culture of violence, watching fights from an early age, and from 13 years old, being thrown into a skip to 'fight it out till the last man standing'. Rather than a means of absolving responsibility, they refer to the 'wrong choices' made, and the stories provide a context for their involvement and responses to the restorative justice process.

The next voices heard are those of the three victim participants who introduce themselves and summarise their experiences. Raymond and Violet share that their two sons were attacked by a gang of youths in the street, leading to the death of their eldest son, Chris. Michelle then tells of the way that her life fell apart after her ex-husband was stabbed in another street attack. Taken from the full conversation to follow, the soundbites draw the audience in and set the tone for the remaining programme. Rather than pitching victim and prisoner against each other, placing their stories side by side attempts to frame them as equally relevant.

The restorative process is then fully introduced by Professor Tanya Byron who presents and mediates the conversation throughout. Byron's role is crucial, as a psychology professional, a media professional, and as a victim of violent crime herself. She introduces herself as 'hosting this session' declaring her own interest in involvement, not only as a psychologist and through her work with disadvantaged young people, but through her own experience, sharing that when she was 15 years old her grandmother had been 'battered to death'. Byron is known for her television and radio work as well as writing regular articles in the national press. As a media personality, her role provides personable, relaxed, listener appeal, while her professional status lends a therapeutic quality to the process. Again focusing on the prisoner perspective, she asks each of the prisoners how they feel in advance of the meeting, with all participants nervous, of not knowing what to expect, and apprehensive about the potential for tears and blame. One participant is particularly defensive and concerned about 'blame', indicating the more authoritarian, retributionist reputation of restorative practice.

The meeting is set up in collaborative and supportive terms, marked by language that suggests and perpetuates mutual respect and trust. Informal introductions and the use of first names for addressing each contributor throughout personalises the process, creating an intimacy and informality that contrasts with formal justice procedures. At each stage in the process, Byron repeats that the crimes described are not those of the prisoners taking part in the programme. The aim is not to attribute blame but for prisoners to begin to understand the impact of crime on victims and families. However, while acknowledging their lack of responsibility for the particular instances, she presses each prisoner on whether the stories had made them think about their own victims. The impact on both victims and prisoners is profound, with all parties surprised at the outcome, revealing that they had little idea of what to expect at the beginning.

Raymond and Violet tell of the random, violent attack on their sons, the extent of Chris' injuries and their reactions to the crime. Their accounts are emotional and extremely difficult for participants and listeners to hear, focusing on the events and the effects on them as parents. The programme rejects the overly dramatic and sentimental tone of much mainstream media coverage of victim issues, making the emotional impact even more intense. Their involvement in the process illustrates the restorative view of many victims of crime, concerned with ways they can prevent other families from being similarly affected, with Violet stressing the need to let go of anger:

> 'My rage is not the answer. It's about restoring them so that they don't come out and do it again ... to anybody.' (Violet, NPR 2012)

Addressing the prisoners directly, they ask for them to recognise that they each have victims, with Raymond stressing the need to recognise them as real people, "Victims have faces, feelings and families ... they're not just a piece of paper in court" (Raymond, NPR 2012). Each account highlights dissatisfaction with existing legal processes for recognising the voice and agency for victims of crime, as reflected in the rise of the victims' movement over recent decades (Strang 2001). As Heather Strang argues, concern for victims has only emerged as a concept in Western democracies in relation to the rising importance of 'law and order' as a political issue: 'For centuries, victims had been the forgotten third parties in a justice system which conceives of criminal behaviour as a matter between the offender and the state, with no formal role for the individuals who suffer the crime' (Strang 2001, p.71).

Victim issues have been used to further political agendas around criminal justice, with mainstream media and campaigners for tougher sentences invoking statements of individual victims as if they were the views of *all* crime victims. Yet as the victims involved in the *Face to Face* programme indicate, views on sentencing and responses to crime are as varied as any other cross-section of the general public (Reeves and Mulley 2000, p.42). Strang presents the victims' movement as a disparate spectrum, broadly divided into victims' rights and victim support (2001, p.72). The US movement has largely been corrupted by the far right as a means of supporting punitive policies (Elias 1990), yet the UK movement leans more towards the support model, epitomised by the status of *Victim Support* as a group for providing assistance services and lobbying for victims' rights. *Victim Support* has increasingly been recognised as an adjunct to the formal justice system, securing a place at the centre of government policy (Crawford 2000) and playing a central role in the development of restorative justice schemes within the court system.

Strang (2001, p.70) highlights the importance of social movements operating outside existing institutions, arguing that those supported by institutions and the state risk being co-opted to varying degrees and in varying forms. Yet where Crawford (2000) suggests that the political status of *Victim Support* has decreased its validity as a social movement, the current commitment to restorative justice highlights the range and importance of the victim role in criminal justice practice.

Rather than the manipulation of the 'ideal victim' concept used to further retributionist policies (Christie 1986), the prison radio partnership project represents the restorative priorities of victims, focusing on changing peoples' lives and stopping others from going through the same experience, "If we can save one of you from reoffending ... the pain will have been worth it" (Raymond, NPR 2012).

Throughout the programme, participants reject the normative labels of 'prisoner' and 'victim', with all referred to by their first names and introduced as people with different experiences of crime. Presenting all parties as real people promotes understanding of the personal impact of crime, while personalising the depiction of crime informs wider public attitudes and responses to crime. When asked how the stories made them feel, Karl, Liam and Adrian all speak about how upset they were, "I feel angry, for Ray and Vi. It is very, very emotional... It's really hard to see, I feel really upset right now" (Karl, NPR 2012).

All express their shock at hearing the stories, indicating that it is the first time they had thought about crime in personal terms. Byron repeats the 'this isn't your crime' message while also pressing them on whether it had made them think about the impact on their own victims. The responses show surprise at considering the pain they had caused:

> 'When you are committing a crime you are not thinking about how it affects your victims.' (Karl, NPR 2012)

> 'I never thought about that person or the pain I caused my victim ... until this day I've never felt this much remorse.' (Liam, NPR 2012)

Michelle's story highlights the complex effects of crime on an individual, family and community level. Her account is very emotional as she describes the aftermath of a random alcohol and cocaine fuelled attack on her husband. He survived being stabbed in the head, yet the emotional impact was more complex, leading to mental health problems, alcohol and drug addiction, and involvement in crime which ultimately led to divorce. The account illustrates the 'ripple effect' of violent crime not only on the individual victim but on a wider level. The issues raised in Michelle's story had particular resonance for the prisoners involved in the programme, relating to "the whole drink and drug fighting culture" that each of them had been involved in to varying degrees:

'It could easily have been me ... it really hit a nerve ... I'm having trouble holding it together right now.' (Karl, NPR 2012)

'I've done a drug fuelled crime, I was on drugs when I committed that crime, and for you to sit there and tell me that story, you find yourself welling up, you don't think about other people. I've done what I've done, I've been to court, I've been to prison, I come out and live my life normal, but people like yourselves, all of you, you're still dealing with that every day ... I've left a permanent mark on that person ... I can honestly say that there's a big feeling of guilt on me now ... more than ever ... I'm happy that I done this.' (Liam, NPR 2012)

Byron describes restorative justice as a process through which people who have been affected by crime come face to face with people who have committed crime, with the aim of the perpetrators understanding the real impact of their actions. She reiterates the idea that offenders are held to account and made to take responsibility while also enabling victims to move forward. Her overview reflects the institutionalised model of restorative justice, yet the language, tone and content of the programme reinforces the principles of trust, respect and collective responsibility which are so often obscured. This is most strikingly demonstrated by Raymond expressing his appreciation, admiration and respect for the prisoners involved in the process:

> 'You're very brave men ... and I think that people listening to this programme should realise that it takes a lot of guts to sit in front of victims of crime, in a small room like this. It's an honour to be in the same room as you.' (Raymond, NPR 2012)

The statement sets the tone of the remaining discussion with 'respect' repeatedly referenced throughout the programme. Once explicitly shown to the prisoners, they mirror the language and behaviour, demonstrated in particular by Liam, who comments on Michelle's bravery in sharing her story.

Respect is a crucial factor in the process of restorative justice and the wider reconstruction of society (Walklate 2008). Sandra Walklate (2008, p.284) highlights the problems of the victim label, arguing that the term is no longer relevant in an increasingly diverse society where difference is to be valued. She presents contemporary definitions as further entrenching divisions of inequality and, while acknowledging that new 'imaginings' are beginning to emerge, argues that significant structural, cultural and political limitations remain: 'Through a 'rhetoric of victimhood' both restorative justice and victimhood become vehicles for state policy, contributing to the culture of control and maintenance of economic relationships' (Walklate 2008, p.283).

She cites Will Hutton's presentation of the demise of the public realm (2002) to illustrate the extent to which the state infrastructure of justice, with aims of equalising opportunity and enlarging individual's capacity for self-respect, has been overtaken by individualism: 'Taken to its limits, a society peopled only by conservative 'unencumbered selves' jealously guarding their individual liberties and privacy, is a denial of the human urge for association and meaning' (Hutton 2002, p.84). For Walklate (2008), the true nature of oppression and opportunities for change lie within these processes, with restoration and reconstruction underpinned by respect for human difference and experience. Where she investigates the victim role in restorative justice, the argument can equally be applied to the involvement of offenders in the process, focusing on the need to treat people with respect, as individuals with personal resources, helping them to make sense of what has happened in their lives.

The *Face to Face* programme frames the restorative justice process through a discourse of respect, treating all involved as individual people with their own equally valid stories and perspectives. Crime impacts on people's lives and, as Walklate controversially suggests, talk of 'victims' and 'criminals' has limitations, invoking the presumed 'special' status associated with victims of crime. Instead, they are complainants in a criminal justice system just as criminals are defendants – they are not necessarily 'good' in opposition to the offender's 'bad' (Walklate 2008, p.284). Within the programme Raymond explicitly raises the issue of respect, breaking down normative, value-laden definitions in a statement that enables the prisoners involved to see themselves and those around them differently:

> 'I'll give you three one word, and that's 'respect', you deserve all the respect we can give you. It takes a lot of guts to come in here and open your heart. You're very brave men, the three of you.' (Raymond, NPR 2012)

Coming into contact with prisoners who are separate from, and not responsible for their own experiences creates a uniquely supportive and rehabilitory process, helping victims to feel empowered to do something positive towards reducing recidivism. Had Raymond, Violet and Michelle been brought together with the perpetrators involved in their own stories, the dynamic would have been different, and the personal distance enabled all involved to respect each other's position. Throughout the process, all express appreciation and respect for each other's time, stories and commitment to the process. For Violet, this is a marked contrast to the court system which "never asked us as victims what we thought or felt" (NPR 2012). For Karl, Liam and Adrian, the programme, prisoner feedback, PRA accounts and my own experience of working in prisons show that prisoners respond far more positively and are far more likely to engage with rehabilitation initiatives when treated with respect and as human beings.

Reflecting wider restorative justice values and practice, the final segments of the documentary focus on moving forward. This includes participant reflections on the process with particular focus on the impact on the prisoners involved, what the experience has done for them, and what they want to do next. One week after the initial meeting, Karl, Liam and Adrian are interviewed separately, with Byron visiting them on the prison wings. The background of general prison noise adds authenticity to their accounts and joining them in their territory breaks down the standard power relations of professional interactions with prisoners. This reinforces the status of their feedback as genuine insight, with all expressing how surprised they were at the emotional effect of the experience. Karl talks of feeling "like crap", of starting to appreciate the personal impact of crime when listening to how people have been hurt while also feeling positive, that he had "done something to make a difference".

Similarly, Adrian talks of feeling "ashamed" and of facing the fact of the emotional pain he caused. Byron points out that his was the most marked change in attitude, and he acknowledges the shift from being defensive to thinking about others. Liam talks of having his eyes opened and of the experience changing his mindset before leaving prison the following week and of being grateful for the opportunity to try and help, "to give something back."

Throughout their reflections, they each refer to varying feelings of 'shame' and 'guilt' in relation to their own victims. To a large extent, the response can be connected to what they feel is expected of prisoners throughout formal criminal justice processes, as well as their role in the programme itself. However, the language used suggests the 'experiencing' of guilt rather than attributing the abstract notion of guilt and culpability. The victims involved are similarly struck by the emotional impact of the experience, with Raymond and Violet talking of being "overwhelmed" by the hope that lives can change because of their son's story. Michelle too talks of being "blown away" by the reactions of the prisoners, feeling that the process may well have resulted in them taking some responsibility for their actions.

> 'It's been an emotional journey, the impact on the lads is powerful. They're all good lads – they deserve another chance.' (Michelle, NPR 2012)

The production and reception of the *Face to Face* documentary marks a major turning point in the development of the PRA, gaining wider support and credibility through facilitating the victim's voice within the prison and punishment debate. While I am in no way suggesting that one radio programme holds the key to the development of restorative justice values and practice in the UK, I do argue that the documentary highlights the need to extend the range of discourse and practice around victims, prisoners and restorative justice. Prison radio challenges mainstream media representations of victims, promoting restorative alternatives through realistic representations of both victims and prisoners and facilitating a constructive dialogue between the two. In addition, the project highlights the importance of principles of reconciliation, reintegration and respect rather than those of individual responsibility through which restorative justice practice has come to be framed. The partnership between the PRA and *Victim Support* demonstrates the importance of the non-profit sector in achieving humanitarian criminal justice reform, showing that innovative prison alternatives can only be developed outside the institutional restrictions of the state through non-profit sector and civil society organisation and activism.

Summary

When discussing the process of establishing the PRA and NPR, founders talk of the need to keep a low public profile and of actively avoiding media attention. For them, the core objective was to develop quality radio that could change the lives of prisoners, an aim that contrasts with the ideas of punishment and retribution that continue to dominate prison discourse. Instead, they talk of remaining focused on building a reputation with the prison audience and relationships with government, prison, non-profit and criminal justice sector partners, keenly aware of the risks posed by outside perceptions of what they were trying to achieve: "We have absolutely positively shied away from engaging in the public arena because of the nervousness of it backfiring, so there hasn't been a major push to engage with the public more broadly about prisoners involved with prison radio" (Hooper 2012).

Here and in the preceding chapter, I have focused on the ways in which the organisation acknowledged and managed the risk of inaccurate assumptions and negative perceptions about the prison radio concept. The PRA experience illustrates the complex and interdependent relationship between news media, perceived public opinion, and the impact on criminal justice policy and practice. Where the PRA media strategy illustrates the potential reputational and operational risks involved in developing prison radio, discussion of the NPR *Face to Face* radio documentary demonstrates a wider acceptance, recognising its contribution to a deeper understanding of prison issues. Both case studies illustrate a strategy that avoids direct engagement with a dominant punitive discourse based on unrealistic representations of prisons and prisoners. Instead, these instances demonstrate potential for building a new, more responsive and representative discourse, reclaiming media power on behalf of prisoners, victims of crime and the wider criminal justice sector.

PART III

Conclusions

8

Ten Years On: Global Themes in Prison Radio Development

On a freezing, rainy day in December 2017, I arrive at the gate of Her Majesty's Prison Brixton in London. Having travelled from the Australian summer, the imposing, grimy brick walls of the 200-year-old prison appear especially bleak against the grey sky. Although it has been three years since my last visit, the gate officer remembers and greets me as I complete the fingerprint and face recognition security checks. I pass through the airlock to meet Andrew Wilkie, PRA Director of Radio and Operations, and it starts to snow as we step outside to the courtyard. He unlocks and locks the multiple doors and high cage-like metal gates for us to cross to the building where National Prison Radio (NPR) occupies a small set of rooms at the end of a narrow windowless corridor.

It is ten years since my first visit to the prison. At that time, the space was a dark dingy storeroom with walls covered in peeling paint and mould. Today, I walk into a bright, bustling creative space, with 15 NPR staff and prisoners working together. The two studios take up the left hand side of the room, NPR staff are busy at computer workstations against the back wall, and the central production area is filled with a new group of prisoners, all editing audio, writing, and talking through ideas with an NPR producer.

Since the 2007 launch of Electric Radio Brixton, the space has evolved into a national radio hub, broadcasting content produced in prisons around the country. Year after year, more people are listening to National Prison Radio, listening for longer, writing in, and getting involved. Reflecting on the distance travelled, PRA Chief Executive Phil Maguire (2016) believes that the service is "more important than it's ever been". He describes a constant feedback loop with listeners and partners, helping the organisation to continually improve, innovate, and understand the needs of the audience.

The PRA evaluation strategy is central to the process. Developed with support from the BBC Radio Audiences Team, ImpetusPEF and Radio Joint Audience Research (RAJAR), the official body in charge of measuring radio audiences in the UK, the methodology reflects broader radio industry practice. For five years, this has involved a rolling schedule of visits to 12 prisons per year to conduct face-to-face surveys with 8% of inmates at each location. The NPR team visits three prisons every three months in a schedule designed to reflect the geographical range and balance of women's, men's and young people's institutions across the estate. In addition, an annual survey printed in the national newspaper for prisoners, *Inside Time*, generates over 700 responses each year. Combined with information gathered from over 6,500 letters that NPR now receives from prisoners each year, the results are collated and published in the annual *PRA Impact Snapshot*. The latest figures show that 97% of prisoners know about National Prison Radio with 72% listening regularly and tuning in for an average 11.4 hours a week (PRA 2017b), results that illustrate the importance of the service to its listeners.

The focus on evaluation and feedback demonstrates the degree to which stakeholder engagement drives the direction of the PRA. In 2016, the PRA celebrated its tenth anniversary. It was a landmark year in which the PRA won the Third Sector 'Charity of the Year' Award, and co-founder Roma Hooper was awarded an OBE in the Queen's 2017 New Year Honours List. The year ended with a major fundraising event at HMP Brixton, run in partnership with the *Letters Live* series of performances which celebrate the power of written correspondence. *Letters from the Inside* was the first time the event was held inside a prison, acknowledging the significance of letter-writing for prisoners as the primary means of maintaining contact with loved ones outside. In an exclusive event, a small audience of 250 people attended the candle-lit prison chapel to see live readings by personalities such as Olivia Coleman, Benedict Cumberbatch and Russell Brand. This included readings of a selection of letters sent to National Prison Radio from actors Matt Berry and Mark Strong, and poet, Kate Tempest, alongside former and serving prisoners. The range of performances showed the individuality of people's stories behind bars, delivered with warmth, emotion and humour. Broadcast live, exclusively on NPR, the presence of the prisoner audience was felt, with one listener commenting "I listened to *Letters Live* last night. It made me smile, laugh and cry. It was inspirational" (PRA 2017b).

The high profile event is one example within a decade of firsts for prison radio, during which the PRA has transformed communication in prisons in England and Wales. Over this time it has gained recognition within the criminal justice, broadcasting, and non-profit sectors, winning numerous industry awards for the quality of its work, including the Longford Prize, two Radio Academy 'Station of The Year' awards, ten Sony Radio Academy Awards, and Gold in the 'Grassroots' category of the Audio Production Awards. Constantly developing its services, the PRA continues to grow, now employing 20 staff involved in content production and organisational development. Together with managing NPR, the organisation produces audio for the BBC and other partners; supports emerging prison radio stations both in the UK and internationally; and is currently developing multimedia services to support prisoners navigate the release process (PRA 2017a).

The PRA launched an independent production company in 2013, building on the success of the *Face to Face* documentary discussed in the previous chapter. PRA Productions specialises in 'making powerful, life-changing audio products' (PRA 2017a) expanding the reach of their audio beyond the prison walls and providing a valuable source of income for the broader work of the organisation. The productions regularly feature on the BBC, including 'Gay on the Inside' with Stephen Fry for BBC Radio 4, and a range of documentaries for BBC World Service, BBC Radio 1, BBC Radio 2, BBC Radio 1Xtra, with other clients including the Samaritans, the Department for Work and Pensions, and the London Probation Trust. Within two years, PRA Productions was nominated twice for 'Indie of the Year' at the Radio Academy's Radio Production Awards, winning the 2014 Silver Award in competition with the best radio producers in the country. In 2016 the venture won Gold in the Social Issues category of the New York International Radio Awards and a coveted Rose d'Or for the BBC Radio 4 programme, 'The Abuse Trial'. Most recently, it was named 'Indie of The Year' at the 2017 Audio Production Awards, with judges describing PRA Productions as a 'clear winner':

> Judges were impressed with the indie's knack for accessing a range of voices and stories that are rarely heard on air. 'The Web Sheikh', a brilliant interview with a mother and her son, who had been radicalised online, and 'A Soundscape with Loan Sharks' were fresh, challenging and insightful. The judges were clearly able to see how their content is changing lives. This indie has grown 54 percent in the past year and is producing some of the most creative and diverse audio on the planet, making them solid gold. (Audio Production Awards 2017)

Such accolades illustrate the PRA's place within the wider broadcast sector, demonstrating an ongoing commitment to quality production and innovative radio. It is a position that indicates the continued importance of radio as a platform for unheard and misrepresented voices, able to challenge the dominant narratives of a homogenised commercial global media landscape.

A continuing belief in the power of radio to change people's lives shapes PRA activity. The impact of NPR for people in prison is demonstrated through annual audience increases and listener feedback. Yet, from the outset, the PRA has recognised the need to develop some kind of continuation service for people leaving prison. Each year, more people are locked up in prisons around the world, with increasing numbers returning to prison in a cycle of reoffending. In the UK, Ministry of Justice statistics show that 44% of adults are reconvicted within one year of release, increasing to 59% for those serving sentences of less than 12 months (Ministry of Justice 2017b). Imprisonment serves to exacerbate the complex disadvantage that leads to criminalisation, separating people even further from any pre-existing support networks. On release, the ability to successfully rebuild lives is dependent on access to support, safe housing, education and employment opportunities, and freely available, regular and consistent services to help with the most prevalent issues of mental illness, domestic violence, and drug and alcohol addiction.

Straightline is the latest PRA initiative in development, designed to support people through life after prison. The traditional linear radio programming format of NPR is the most effective means of reaching prisoners, isolated from the internet, computers and mobile telephones. Yet in the outside world, people interact with radio differently. *Straightline* is designed to reflect the changing ways in which radio is made, shared and accessed. For instance, a NPR music show of the same name is now shared on Mixcloud for people outside to hear song requests, helping to maintain the family and social connections vital for successful reintegration.

The broader vision is shown by the recently launched *Straightline* website, aimed at people who have been in prison, have been convicted, or are at risk of criminalisation. It provides a range of on-demand, audio and video content based on real experiences and providing practical advice and guidance.

Building on the principles of prison radio, it is a multimedia platform that places those with lived prison experience at the centre of design, development and production. This is illustrated through a recent pilot phase involving the production of seven high quality short films in which people told their stories. The films were designed for smartphone viewing and tested through a focus group of former prisoners. While the films were seen as inspirational, feedback highlighted a need for more practical content to support pathways outside prison. Currently, two digital production hubs are being established outside HMPs Brixton and Styal to equip former prisoners with the skills to become campaign producers and smartphone contributors.

Contemporary significance

In 2017, the annual Longford Lecture was broadcast live for the first time on National Prison Radio, to prisoners across the UK. Established in honour of politician and penal reform campaigner, Frank Longford, the lectures provide a platform for discussion on critical issues of social and prison reform. The event also celebrates those working for change within the criminal justice sector through the award of the annual Longford Prize. This year's winner was *Safe Ground*, the performing arts group helping prisoners to build and maintain family relationships. Working to reduce the stigma faced by the families of people in prison, *Safe Ground* recognises the need to create alternatives to traditional punishment and exclusion which have been proven to be so ineffective and damaging (Safe Ground 2018). As Chief Executive Officer Charlotte Weinberg so accurately states on receiving the award, "Justice is a structural and systemic issue as well as being a personal and a political issue" (National Prison Radio 2017).

There is a worsening and unrelenting global prison population crisis, shaped by a 'tough on crime' political rhetoric and perpetuated by a dominant media discourse of drama and fear.

The use of imprisonment has rapidly increased over the past three decades, with the latest figures showing in excess of 11 million people in prison worldwide (Walmsley 2016). The United States holds around one-fifth of the world's prisoners, with a prison population that has quadrupled from around half a million in 1980 to a peak of over 2.3 million in 2008 (Jacobson et al 2017). The US corporate strategy of mass incarceration has become the model for prison systems around the world. It dominates the penal landscape, not only through the direct marketing of products and services to other governments, but through the powerful influence it wields in shaping the style of state punishment in different jurisdictions (Davis 2003).

For instance, increasingly punitive policies, the adoption of mandatory minimum sentencing, and the expansion of prison privatisation modelled by the US have led to the dramatic escalation of prison populations in Australia and New Zealand, with figures for the Oceania region increasing by 60% between 2000 and 2015 (Walmsley 2016). It is a process that has seen the exponential and disproportionate rise in the imprisonment of First Nations Peoples, with devastating effects on entire communities and indicating vast inequalities of justice. Where Aboriginal and Torres Strait Islander peoples make up around 2% of the adult population in Australia, they represent over 27% of adult prisoners (Australian Bureau of Statistics 2017). Similarly, Māori make up only 14.6% of the adult population in Aotearoa New Zealand, but a staggering 51% of the prison population (Wright 2016).

Within this context of systemic and structural crisis, prison radio is more significant than ever. As shown throughout this study, radio can be a powerful platform for prisoner voices, able to improve understanding about the personal and social effects of imprisonment, and facilitate conversations about prison alternatives. Where prison has become accepted as an undisputed and inevitable consequence of crime, increasing incarceration and reoffending rates show that it fails to reduce crime. Instead, it serves to further criminalise, brutalise and exclude those already at the margins of society, despite the best efforts of the individuals and organisations working to create a more humane and constructive space.

The culture of fear and violence in prisons described at the beginning of this book shows no signs of abating. In England and Wales, prisoners and staff are less safe than they have been at any other point since records began, with more self-inflicted deaths, incidents of self-harm, and reported assaults than ever before (Prison Reform Trust 2017a). It is a situation underpinned and exacerbated by chronic levels of overcrowding, understaffing and underfunding. With the highest imprisonment rate in Western Europe, the prison population has risen by 82% in the last 30 years. The Summer 2017 Bromley Briefings produced by the Prison Reform Trust show that 76 of the 117 prisons across the estate are overcrowded, holding 9,496 people more than they were designed to (Prison Reform Trust 2017a). At the same time, the number of frontline operational staff employed in the public prison estate has fallen by over 25% in the last seven years, placing additional pressure on an already overstretched system.

Global prison expansion is connected to the agendas of politicians, the profit motives of corporations, and media representations of crime, all associated with the race, class and gender of those most likely to be punished (Davis 2003, p.112). Rather than an inevitable response to rising crime rates, mass incarceration is central to the rise of global capitalism. Again, Wacquant (2009, p.309) provides a vivid account, describing an expansive, intrusive, and proactive penal apparatus as a central tenant of neoliberalism, reasserting the authority of the state, deepening divisions in society, and extending the cultural trope of individual responsibility.

Politicians, corporations, and mass media all have a vested interest in perpetuating the notion that crime is out of control, ensuring a steady supply of prisoners in order to justify and strengthen the growth of the prison industrial complex. As such, the dominant prison discourse obscures the understanding of the personal and social effects of prison expansion, and blocks debate about prison alternatives. As Anderson argues, prison media plays a critical role in producing alternative discourses on crime and punishment (2012). When run independently, by and for people with lived prison experience, radio is a powerful means of opening up the conversation about the strategies that work, demystifying the prison experience, and raising awareness about the realities of prison life.

Such work is central to the development of decarceration strategies, able to raise awareness and support for the more restorative, community-based solutions proven to be more effective for reducing reoffending. Returning once more to Angela Davis's (2003) powerful argument for prison abolition, she stresses the need to disarticulate the conceptual link between crime and punishment in order to develop a more nuanced understanding of the social role of punishment. The challenges faced by criminal justice practitioners and activists are uniquely complicated in the era of the prison industrial complex. She argues that the traditional rhetoric of reform serves to strengthen an unworkable and unfair system. Yet equally, it is important to acknowledge the efforts of those working from within the system to create a more humane and habitable environment. The major challenge lies in balancing the need to improve conditions for the people in prison, without bolstering the permanence of the prison system (Davis 2003, p.102).

From this environment of global mass incarceration, a growing international movement of prison radio is emerging, with current projects operating in countries as diverse as Ecuador, Hungary, Norway, and Trinidad and Tobago. Formats differ, reflecting the unique issues faced within each correctional jurisdiction. For instance, *Radio Focus* grew in response to the high levels of people suffering from learning disabilities and attention deficit disorders in Israeli prisons, recognising radio training and production as a creative way to address the problems faced. Equally, changes in audio recording and production technology have increased the range of content made in prisons. For instance, *Radio Fri* is a Swedish community radio programme made by young people with experience of prison, crime and addiction, and is produced by two teams based inside and outside prison. In the US, critically acclaimed podcast *Ear Hustle* is made at San Quentin State Prison, California. Produced in the prison's media lab, the team works 'to produce stories that are sometimes difficult, often funny and always honest, offering a nuanced view of people living within the American prison system' (Ear Hustle 2018).

The organisation, content and ways in which audio in prisons is made, shared and listened to varies. Yet without exception, all present their aims in terms of the transformative effects for those involved and the importance of adding prisoner voices to the discussion and debate on crime and punishment. In response to growing interest and requests for support from around the globe, the PRA has established *Prison Radio International*. Radio may well be tolerated and supported within different penal systems, but activity is low on the list of operational priorities for prison staff and management. As such, practitioners are often isolated and under-resourced. The first international forum was held at the 2016 PRA annual conference, bringing together representatives from Scotland, Hungary, Sweden, Australia, Israel, and Trinidad and Tobago. Through formalising and building an international community, the aim is to learn from each other, share best practice, and build strength through collaboration.

The prisoner voice

This study set out to examine the beginnings of prison radio in the UK. As the most established organisation of its kind to date, the PRA story provides a useful case study for the development of emerging activity worldwide. The work focused on the complex contexts that influenced the growth of a particular form of radio for prisoners at a particular time, and presents the PRA and NPR as products of multiple, contradictory, political, economic and social conditions. Ultimately, I argue that prison radio is defined by the motivations, values and approach of the people involved in the process. PRA founders have remained committed to the original aim of changing the lives of prisoners through radio by navigating and negotiating rapidly shifting institutional and governmental environments. It is a story that highlights transferable themes which can be applied to future development in the field. These include commitments to: prisoner participation; the production of high quality content; ongoing evaluation and consultation; organic and mutually beneficial partnerships; and a focus on maintaining organisational independence.

The research findings highlight the ways in which participants remained focused on the production of quality radio while building key relationships and managing misconceptions about what they were trying to achieve. PRA founders all express a commitment to recognising, respecting and responding to the needs of an underserved and underrepresented audience in order to produce quality, relevant and impactful radio. This approach extends to recognition of the needs of all stakeholders, working flexibly and collaboratively to demonstrate the benefits of activity to a range of partners. The independence of the PRA is central, together with a flexible approach to bringing together and balancing stakeholder aims.

The unique impact and potential of prison radio is dependent on the PRA's ability to provide prisoners with a voice, representing the needs of a complex and misunderstood target audience (Wilkie 2012). Throughout the interviews, PRA participants all continue to be driven by a belief in the potential of radio to change lives, and recognise prisoner participation as central to the provision of a relevant and effective radio service, whether through direct presentation and production, listener feedback, or music requests. Unlike other radio stations, listeners are unable to participate in programming through telephone, text message, email or social media. Instead, NPR listeners write letters to the station to make music requests and to share how they are using time inside, and their hopes for life outside.

This is most effectively demonstrated through Andrew Wilkie's account of a letter sent to NPR. A woman prisoner wrote about her best friend who had been in prison with her and had been released two weeks previously. They had made plans for the future and were feeling positive about life on release. Within a week she received a letter from the friend saying that she was doing well. Yet later on the same day, a prison officer visited her cell to let her know that her friend had overdosed and died. The heartbreaking story reflects one of the key drug education messages regularly broadcast through NPR, and the letter reiterates the need to get the message out about the dangers of overdosing after going through detox. As Wilkie states, the decision to share her story with NPR is significant:

> 'It's an incredibly sad story, but the fact that she chose to write to us, and wanted us to be the people to communicate this story proves to me that what we do has a real impact on the people who listen. She took the time to write that letter to us. She wrote to us because she trusts us and she knows that we are there to represent her, and knows that we have the prisoners' best interests at heart – we don't want them to go out and reoffend or to go out and start taking drugs again. And voices like hers, giving that warning, are really powerful. It's a powerful letter to receive. Every so often we'll have a moment like that, and that's just a really concrete example of why I think it's so valuable.' (Wilkie 2012)

The account encapsulates a relationship that defines prison radio, framed in terms of understanding, empathy and mutual respect. For the majority of the general public, who have little or no direct experience of prison, it functions as an abstract site for depositing criminals, undesirables and 'evil-doers'. This ideological function is convenient, relieving us of the responsibility of engaging with the problems of society (Davis 2003, p.16), particularly the problems produced by global capitalism and the spread of individualisation which serve to depersonalise and dehumanise the prison position. Yet the aims and motivations of those involved in establishing the PRA and NPR demonstrate an enduring commitment to social justice, representing a growing, wider concern about the prison problem.

Again, the NPR broadcast of the 2017 Longford Lecture illustrates this position. Hosting the event, PRA Trustee and television journalist Jon Snow initiates a round of applause to welcome the prison audience in a 'sense of spiritual unity' (NPR 2017). Film director and social activist Ken Loach is the guest speaker for the year, delivering an impassioned speech on the devastating effects of increasingly punitive social welfare policy on poverty, homelessness, mental illness, life expectancy and imprisonment. The lecture is followed by the comments from the audience, sharing experiences of disadvantage and struggles with those in power and authority. The prison audience is referenced throughout with one former prisoner expressing the extent to which the comments would be resonating with listeners in their cells. Throughout the programme, the theme is one of solidarity with those suffering behind bars, one which extends to the officers and workers struggling within an unfair and unworkable system.

In a uniquely isolated environment, radio is a uniquely effective medium. The personal qualities of radio listening add to its usefulness as a means of connection and communication, helping people to feel part of a constructive and supportive community. Equally, it is a practical and increasingly accessible way of giving people a voice, providing a platform to discuss the issues that matter to them in their own terms. Criminalised people are among the most silenced and misrepresented in society, yet they can contribute perspectives and experiences that are vital for understanding and addressing recidivism.

In this study, I set out to investigate the early history of the PRA in order to understand the ways in which radio came to be used, supported and encouraged in prisons in a particular time and place. Through a detailed examination of the political, economic and cultural context, I connect PRA growth to significant changes in the ways in which broadcasting, punishment and social welfare are organised and conceptualised and argue that the development of an independent radio service made by and for people in prison represents resistance against the ongoing process of marketisation and managerialism across all three arenas. Ten years on, and the combined forces of global commercial media power and the global prison economy continue to intensify. Prison radio has an increasingly significant role to play in disrupting the dominant prison discourse, challenging punitive retributionist, business-driven attitudes to prisoners and prisons, and rehumanising the punishment debate. The PRA story shows that, even where profit has come to overwhelm all areas of social functioning, people still manage to find creative ways to work within the system to change the lives of others and fight for the voices of the hidden to be heard.

References

Adorno, T.W. and Horkheimer, M., 1991. *The Culture Industry*. pp.98–106. JM Bernstein.

Allan, T., 2006. 'Prison Radio versus Panopticism'. *Variant*, vol.26, pp.21–2.

Anderson, H., 2012. *Raising the Civil Dead: prisoners and community radio*. Peter Lang.

Andrew, J., 2007. 'Prisons, the Profit Motive and Other Challenges to Accountability'. *Critical Perspectives on Accounting*, vol.18, pp.877–904.

Audio Production Awards, 2017. www.audioproductionawards.co.uk/index.php/entering

Australian Bureau of Statistics, 2017. *Aboriginal and Torres Strait Islander Prisoner Characteristics*.

Atton, C., 2001. *Alternative Media*. Sage.

Barak, G., 1988. 'Newsmaking criminology: Reflections of the media, intellectuals, and crime'. *Justice Quarterly*, vol.5, no.4, pp.565–587.

Bastow, S., 2013. *Governance, Performance, and Capacity Stress: The Chronic Case of Prison Crowding*. Palgrave Macmillan.

Bentham, J., 2008 [1791]. *Panopticon or the Inspection House*. Dodo Press.

Berman, G. and Dar, A., 2013. *Prison Population Statistics*. House of Commons Library.

Born, G., 2004. *Uncertain Vision: Birt, Dyke and the Reinvention of the BBC*. Vintage.

Born, G., 2003. 'From Reithian Ethic to Managerial Discourse Accountability and Audit at the BBC Georgina Born'. *Javnost-The Public*, vol.10, no.3, pp.63–80.

Born, G. and Prosser, T., 2001. 'Culture and consumerism: Citizenship, public service broadcasting and the BBC's fair trading obligations'. *The Modern Law Review*, vol.64, no.5, pp.657–687.

Bottoms, A., 1995. 'The philosophy and politics of punishment and sentencing.' In A. Bottoms, C. Clarkson and R. Morgan (eds) *The politics of sentencing reform*, pp.17–49. Oxford University Press.

Box, S., 1983. *Power, Crime and Mystification*. Tavistock, London.

Brecht, B., 1979. 'Radio as a Means of Communication: A Talk on the Function of Radio'. *Screen*, vol.20, no.3–4, pp.24–28.

Brownlee, I., 1998. 'New Labour – New Penology? Punitive Rhetoric and the Limits of Managerialism in Criminal Justice Policy'. *Journal of Law and Society*, vol.32, no.3, pp.313–335.

Bryans, S., Martin, C. and Walker, R., 2002. *Prisons and the Voluntary Sector: A Bridge into the Community*. Waterside Press.

Buckley, S., 2000. 'Radio's New Horizons: Democracy and Popular Communication in the Digital Age'. *International Journal of Cultural Studies*, vol.3, no.2, pp.180–187.

Carpentier, N., Lie, R. and Servaes, J., 2003. 'Community media: Muting the democratic media discourse?' *Continuum*, vol.17, no.1, pp.51–68.

Carrabine, E., Iganski, P., Lee, M., Plummer, K. and South, N., 2004. *Criminology, A Sociological Introduction*. Routledge.

Cheliotis, L.K., 2010. 'The ambivalent consequences of visibility: Crime and prisons in the mass media'. *Crime, Media, Culture*, vol.6, no.2, pp.169–184.

Clements, P., 2004. 'The rehabilitative role of arts education in prison: Accommodation or enlightenment?' *International Journal of Art & Design Education*, vol.23, no.2, pp.169–178.

Clinks, 2014. *More Than a Provider: the role of the voluntary sector in the commissioning of offender services*.

Collins, M., 1988. 'Prison education: A substantial metaphor for adult education practice'. *Adult education quarterly*, vol.38, no.2, pp.101–110.

Crawford, A., 2000. 'Salient Themes Towards a Victim Perspective and the Limitations of Restorative Justice: Some concluding comments'. In A. Crawford and J. Goodey, J. (eds) *Integrating a Victim Perspective Within Criminal Justice: International Debates*. Ashgate.

REFERENCES

Crissell, A., 2002. *An Introductory History of British Broadcasting.* Routledge.

Christie, N., 1986. 'The Ideal Victim'. In E.A. Fattah (ed) *From Crime Policy to Victim Policy*, pp. 17–30. Palgrave Macmillan.

Damaska, M. R., 1968. 'Adverse Legal Consequences of Conviction and Their Removal: A Comparative Study'. *Journal of Criminal Law, Criminology and Police Science*, vol.59, no.3, pp.347–360.

Davis, A.Y., 2003. *Are Prisons Obsolete?* Open Media.

De Beaumont, G. and De Tocqueville, A., 1833. *On the Penitentiary System in the United States: and its application in France.* Carey, Lea & Blanchard.

De Mesmaecker, V., 2010. 'Building social support for restorative justice through the media: is taking the victim perspective the most appropriate strategy?' *Contemporary Justice Review*, vol.13, no.3, pp.239–267.

Di Ronco, A., 2016. 'Media representation of regulated incivilities: Relevant actors, problems, solutions and the role played by experts in the Flemish press'. *Criminology & Criminal Justice*, vol.16, no.5, pp.585–601.

Douglas, S.J., 2004. *Listening in: Radio and the American Imagination.* University of Minnesota Press.

Dreisinger, B., 2017. *Incarceration Nations: A Journey to Justice in Prisons around the World.* Other Press.

Dubber, A., 2014. *Radio in the Digital Age.* John Wiley & Sons.

Ear Hustle, 2018. https://www.earhustlesq.com/

Elias, R., 1990. 'Which Victim Movement? The Politics of Victim Policy'. In A. Lurigio, W. Skogan and R. Davis (eds) *Victims of Crime, Problems, Policies and Programs.* Sage.

Fairclough, N., 2000. *New Labour, New Language?* Routledge.

Feeley, M. and Simon, J., 1992. 'The New Penology: Notes on the Emerging Strategy of Corrections and its Implications'. *Criminology*, vol.30, no.4, pp.449–474.

Fisher, M., 2008. 'Stand up for comedy in prisons', *Guardian*, 25 November.

Foucault, M., 2002. *The Archaeology of Knowledge.* Routledge Classics.

Foucault, M., 1991. *Discipline and Punish: the Birth of the Prison*. Penguin Books.

Garland, D., 2001. *The Culture of Control*. Oxford University Press.

Garland, D., 1997. "Governmentality' and the Problem of Crime: Foucault, Criminology, Sociology'. *Theoretical Criminology*, vol.1, no.2, pp.173–214.

Garland, D., 1990. *Punishment and Modern Society: A Study in Social Theory*. University of Chicago Press.

Garland, D. and Sparks, R., 2000. *Criminology and Social Theory*. Oxford University Press.

Garrett, P.M., 2014. 'Neoliberalism and 'Welfare' in the shadow of the prison'. In R. Sheehan and J. Ogloff (eds) *Working within the Forensic Paradigm: Cross-discipline approaches for policy and practice* (Vol. 22). Routledge.

Giddens, A., 1998. *The Third Way: The Renewal of Social Democracy*. Polity Press, Cambridge, England.

Goodman, D., 2011. *Radio's Civic Ambition: American broadcasting and democracy in the 1930s*. Oxford University Press.

Gray, P., 2005. The politics of risk and young offenders' experiences of social exclusion and restorative justice. *British Journal of Criminology*, vol.45, no.6, pp.938–957.

Gray-Felder, D., 2001. 'Foreword'. In A.G. Dagron (ed) *Making Waves: stories of participatory communication for social change*. Rockefeller Foundation.

Green, D.A., 2009. Feeding Wolves: punitiveness and culture. *European Journal of Criminology*, vol.6, no.6, pp.517–536.

Greer, C., 2007. *News Media, Victims and Crime*. In P. Davies, P. Francis and C. Greer (eds) *Victims, Crime and Society*. Sage.

Hallin, D.C., 2008. *Neoliberalism, Social Movements and Change in Media Systems in the Late Twentieth Century*. In D. Hesmondhalgh and J. Toynebee (eds) *The Media and Social Theory*. Routledge.

Hartley, J., 2000. 'Radiocracy – Sound and Citizenship'. *International Journal of Cultural Studies,* vol.3, no.2, pp.153–159.

Hajkowski, T., 2010. *The BBC and National Identity in Britain 1922–53*. Manchester University Press.

REFERENCES

Hall, S., 1997. *Representation: Cultural Representation and Signifying Practises.* Sage.

Hall, S., 1980. *Drifting into a Law and Order Society.* Cobden Trust.

Hall, S., Critcher, C., Jefferson, T., Clarke, J. and Roberts, B., 2013 [1978]. *Policing the Crisis: Mugging, the State and Law and Order.* Palgrave Macmillan.

Harcourt, B.E., 2010. 'Neoliberal penality: A brief genealogy'. *Theoretical Criminology*, vol.14, no.1, pp.74–92.

Harrison, J. and Wessels, B., 2005. 'A new public service communication environment? Public service broadcasting values in the reconfiguring media'. *New Media & Society*, vol.7, no.6, pp.834–853.

Hendy, D., 2000. *Radio in the Global Age.* Polity Press.

Hesmondhalgh, D., 2002. *The Cultural Industries.* Sage.

HM Inspectorate of Prisons, 2017. *Annual Report 2016–17.* Crown Copyright.

Hood, S., 1979. 'Brecht on Radio'. *Screen*, vol.20, no.3/4, pp.16–23.

Hooper, R., 2002, 'The Contribution of the Voluntary Sector in the Penal System'. In S. Bryans, C. Martin and R. Walter (eds) *Prisons and the Voluntary Sector: A Bridge into the Community.* Waterside Press.

Hooper, R., 2012. Interview with PRA Chair and Founder, 27 November.

Home Office, 2004. *Reducing Re-offending National Action Plan.*

Howitt, D., 1998. *Crime, the Media, and the Law.* Wiley, Chichester.

Howkins, J., 2002. *The Creative Economy: How people make money from ideas.* Penguin UK.

Hutton, W., 2002. *The World We're In.* Little Brown, London.

Incite!, 2017. *The Revolution Will Not be Funded: Beyond the non-profit industrial complex.* Duke University Press.

Inglis, T., 1997. Empowerment and emancipation. *Adult Education Quarterly*, vol.48, no.1, pp.3–17.

Jacka, E., 2003. '"Democracy as Defeat" The Impotence of Arguments for Public Service Broadcasting'. *Television & New Media*, vol.4, no.2, pp.177–191.

Jacobson, J., Heard, C., and Fair, H. 2017. *Prison: Evidence of its use and over-use from around the world*. Fair Trials & The Institute for Criminal Policy Research, Birkbeck, University of London.

Jewkes, Y., 2015. *Media and Crime*. Sage.

Jewkes, Y. and Reisdorf, B.C., 2016. 'A brave new world: The problems and opportunities presented by new media technologies in prisons'. *Criminology & Criminal Justice*, vol.16, no.5, pp.534–551.

Jewkes, Y. and Johnston, H., 2009. 'Cavemen in an Era of Speed-of-Light Technology': Historical and Contemporary Perspectives on Communication within Prisons. *The Howard Journal of Criminal Justice,* vol.48, pp.132–143.

Kay, J., 2009. 'Prisons Excusive: Con Air, Lags' Radio Station to Cost Public £2m', *The Sun,* 20 January.

Kirkpatrick, B., 2011. '"A Blessed Boon": Radio, Disability, Governmentality and the Discourse of the "Shut-In" 1920–1930'. *Critical Studies in Media Communication,* vol. 29, no.3, pp.165–184.

Kivel, P., 2017. 'Social Service or Social Change?' In Incite! (ed) *The Revolution Will Not be Funded: Beyond the non-profit industrial complex*. Duke University Press.

Klare, H.J., 1973. *People in Prison*. Pitman.

Knight, V., 2015. 'Some observations on the digital landscape of prisons today'. *Prison Service Journal*, vol. 220, pp.3–10.

Lacey, N., 2010. 'Differentiating Among Penal States', *The British Journal of Sociology*, vol.61, no.4, pp.778–794.

Lacey, N., 2008. *The Prisoners' Dilemma: political economy and punishment in contemporary democracies*. Cambridge University Press.

Leadbeater, C., 1997. *The Rise of the Social Entrepreneur.* Demos.

Leadbeater, C. and Oakley, K., 2005. 'Why Cultural Entrepreneurs Matter'. In J. Hartley (ed) *Creative Industries.* Blackwell Publishing.

Leadbeater, C. and Oakley, K., 1999. *The Independents: Britain's New Cultural Entrepreneur.* Demos.

Lewis, P.M., 2000. 'Private Passion, Public Neglect: The Cultural Status of Radio'. *International Journal of Cultural Studies*, vol. 3, no. 2, pp.160–167.

REFERENCES

Lewis, P.M. and Booth J., 1989. *The Invisible Medium*. London: Macmillan.

Maguire, P., 2016. Interview with PRA Chief Executive, 7 September.

Maguire, P., 2012. Interview with PRA Chief Executive, 28 November.

Mason, P., 2007. 'Misinformation, myth and distortion: how the press construct imprisonment in Britain'. *Journalism Studies*, vol. 8, no.3, pp.481–496.

Mason, P., 2006. 'Lies, distortion and what doesn't work: Monitoring prison stories in the British media'. *Crime, Media, Culture*, vol.2, no.3, pp.251–267.

McAdam, D., 1986. 'Recruitment to High-Risk Activism: The case of freedom summer'. *American Journal of Sociology*, vol.92, no.1, pp.64–90.

McCarthy, J., 2012. Interview with former PRA Project Coordinator. 12 December.

McDermott, N., 2008. 'A Sick Joke: terrorist signs up for comedy classes at top security prison', *Daily Mail*, 22 November.

McDowell, P., 2012. Interview with PRA Trustee and former Governor of HMP Brixton. 29 November.

McClure, K., 1992. 'On the Subject of Rights: Pluralism, Plurality and Political Identity'. In C. Mouffe (ed) *Dimensions of Radical Democracy – Pluralism, Citizenship, Community*. Verso.

Meadows, M., Forde S., Ewart, J. and Foxwell, K., 2007. *Community Media Matters – an Audience Study of the Australian Community Radio Sector*. Griffith University.

Mills, S., 2003. *Michel Foucault*. Routledge, London and New York.

Ministry of Justice, 2017a. *Safety in Custody Statistics Bulletin, England and Wales, Deaths in prison custody to June 2017, Assaults and Self-Harm to March 2017*. National Statistics.

Ministry of Justice, 2017b. Proven Reoffending Statistics July 2014 to June 2015.

Ministry of Justice, 2013. *The Story of the Prison Population 1993–2012 England and Wales*.

Mouffe, C., 1992. 'Democratic Citizenship and the Political Community'. In C. Mouffe (ed) *Dimensions of Radical Democracy – Pluralism, Citizenship, Community.* Verso.

Morison, J., 2000. 'The Government-Voluntary Sector Compacts: Governance, Governmentality, and Civil Society'. *Journal of Law and Society*, vol.27, no.1, pp.98–132.

Munshi, S. and Willse, C., 2017. 'Foreword'. In Incite! (ed) *The Revolution Will Not be Funded: Beyond the non-profit industrial complex.* Duke University Press.

National Council of Nonprofit Associations, 2000. *The United States Non-Profit Sector: Annual Report.* Washington, DC.

National Prison Radio (NPR) 2017. *Longford Lecture 2017 with Ken Loach.* https://soundcloud.com/prisonradioassociation/longford-lecture-2017-with-ken-loach

NPR, 2012. *Face to Face*, https://soundcloud.com/prisonradioassociation/face-to-face-national-prison-radio

Newsworks, 2016a, 'Daily Mail', www.newsworks.org.uk/Daily-Mail

Newsworks, 2016b, 'The Sun', www.newsworks.org.uk/The-Sun

Nolan, D., 2006. 'Media, citizenship and governmentality: Defining "the public" of public service broadcasting'. *Social Semiotics*, vol.16, no.2, pp.225–242.

Open Justice, 2017. 'The truth about prisons', http://open.justice.gov.uk/reoffending/prisons/

Plunkett, J., 2009. 'Brixton Prison Radio 'A Daily Mail Story Waiting to Happen', says Governor', *Guardian,* 30 June.

Prison Radio Association (PRA) 2017a. https://prison.radio/

PRA, 2017b. Impact Snapshot.

PRA, 2016. National Prison Radio Induction Handbook.

PRA, 2006. *Making Waves Behind Bars.* Audio CD.

Prison Reform Trust, 2017a. *Prison: The Facts. Bromley Briefings, Summer 2017.*

Prison Reform Trust, 2017b. *Why Focus on Reducing Women's Imprisonment?* PRT Briefing, February 2017.

Prison Reform Trust, 2013. *Charities say computers can transform prisoner rehabilitation.*

REFERENCES

Reeves, H. and Mulley, K., 2000. 'The New Status of Victims in the UK: Opportunities and Threats'. In A. Crawford and J. Goodey (eds) *Integrating a Victim Perspective within Criminal Justice*. Ashgate.

Restorative Justice Council, 2012. *Offenders Meet Victims for Pioneering Radio Programme*. www.restorativejustice.org.uk/news/offenders_meet_victims_for_pioneering_radio programme

Rodriguez, C., 2001. *Fissures in the Mediascape: An International Study of Citizens' Media*. Hampton Press Communication Series.

Robinson, M., 2012. Interview with PRA Founder, 28 November.

Rose, N., 2000. 'Community, Citizenship, and the Third Way'. *American Behavioural Scientist*, vol.43, no.9, pp.1395–1411.

Ryan, M. and Ward T., 1989. *Privatization and the Penal System: the American Experience and the Debate in Britain*. Open University Press, London.

Safe Ground, 2018. http://www.safeground.org.uk/

Saxton, J. and Kanemura, R., 2015. *Understanding Charities Group September*. nfpsynergy.net

Scales, R., 2008. 'Radio Broadcasting, Disabled Veterans, and the Politics of National Recovery in Interwar France'. *French Historical Studies*, vol.31, no.4, pp.643–678.

Scannell, P., 1989. 'Public Service Broadcasting and Modern Public Life'. *Media Culture Society*, vol.11, no.2, pp.135–166. http://mcs.sagepub.com/content/11/2/135.short

Seppings, C., 2015. *The Rehabilitative Role of Ex-Offenders as Peer Mentors*. The Churchill Trust.

Sim, J., 2009. *Punishment and Prisons: Power and the Carceral State*. Sage.

Sim, J., 1994. 'Tougher than the rest? Men in Prison'. In T. Newburn and B. Stanko (eds) *Just boys doing the business?: Men, Masculinities and Crime*. Routledge.

Smith, A., 2017. 'Preface'. In Incite! (ed) *The Revolution Will Not be Funded: Beyond the non-profit industrial complex*. Duke University Press.

Solomon, E., 2005. 'Is the Press the Real Power Behind Punitivism?' *Criminal Justice Matters*, vol.59, no.1, pp.34–35.

Sokolowski, S.W., 1996. 'Show me the Way to the Next Worthy Deed: Towards a Microstructural Theory of Volunteering and Giving'. *Voluntas: International Journal of Voluntary and Nonprofit Organisations*, vol.7, no.3, pp.259–278.

Sparks, R., 2001. 'The Media, Populism, Public Opinion and Crime'. *Criminal Justice Matters*, vol.43, no.1, pp.6–7.

Strang, H., 2001. 'The Crime Victim Movement as a Force in Civil Society'. In H. Strang and J. Braithwaite (eds), *Restorative Justice and Civil Society*, Cambridge University Press, pp.69–82.

Strang, H. and Braithwaite, J., 2001. *Restorative Justice and Civil Society*. Cambridge University Press.

Sullivan, D. and Tifft, L., 2008. *Handbook of Restorative Justice*. Routledge.

Tacchi, J., 2000. 'The Need for Radio Theory in the Digital Age'. *International Journal of Cultural Studies*, vol. 3, no.2, pp.289–298.

Taylor, T.D., 2002. 'Music and the rise of radio in 1920s America: Technological imperialism, socialization, and the transformation of intimacy'. *Historical Journal of Film, Radio and Television*, vol.22, no.4, pp.425–443.

The Care Leavers Association, 2013. *Practice Guidance for Criminal Justice Practitioners*.

Third Sector, 2012. 'Third Sector Excellence Awards 2012: Charity Partnership - Winner: Prison Radio Association with Victim Support', 27 September. https://www.thirdsector.co.uk/

Tighe, S., 2016. 'Prisoners allowed access to adult films and internet', BBC News Online, 22 April. www.bbc.com/news/world-europe-36067653

Tilley, K., 2012. Interview with PRA Trustee and former Director of Operations. 28 November.

Van Vuuren, K., 2001. 'Beyond the Studio: a Case Study of Community Radio and Social Capital'. *Australian Community Broadcasting Series*, vol.1, no.4.

Wacquant, L., 2010. 'Crafting the neoliberal state: Workfare, prisonfare, and social insecurity'. *Sociological Forum*, vol.25, no.2, pp.197–220). Blackwell Publishing.

REFERENCES

Wacquant, L., 2009. *Punishing the Poor: The Neoliberal Government of Social Insecurity.* Duke University Press.

Wacquant, L., 2003. 'The Penalization of Poverty and the Rise of Neo-liberalism'. *Capítulo Criminológico*, vol.31, no.1, pp.7–22.

Walklate, S., 2008. 'Changing Boundaries of the 'Victim' in Restorative Justice – So who is the victim now?' In D. Sullivan and L. Tifft (eds) *Handbook of Restorative Justice: A Global Perspective*, Routledge, p.273.

Walmsley, R., 2016. *World Prison Population List.* World Prison Brief and Institute for Criminal Policy Research.

Waltz, M., 2005. *Alternative and Activist Media.* Edinburgh University Press.

Wilkie, A., 2012. Interview with PRA Director of Radio and Operations, 28 November.

Wilkinson, K. and Davidson, D., 2008. *An Evaluation of the Prison Radio Association's Activity: The West Midlands Prison Radio Taster Project.* The Hallam Centre for Community Justice, Sheffield Hallam University.

Wilson, J., 2000. 'Volunteering'. *Annual Review of Sociology*, vol.26, pp.215–240.

Wright, T., 2016. 'Māori prison rates at record levels', News Hub, 23 October. www.newshub.co.nz/home/new-zealand/2016/10/maori-prison-rates-at-record-levels.html

Index

A

Aboriginal and Torres Strait Islander people, Australia 143, 169
Adorno, Theodor 29, 30
adult education 106, 108–110
  see also prison education
Allan, Tom 54–55
alternative media 28
Anderson, Heather 20, 21, 27–28, 171
Andrew, Jane 41
Anne Peaker Unit for Arts and Offenders 108
Annual Report (HM Inspectorate of Prisons, 2017) 49, 50
Aotearoa New Zealand, prison population growth 169
armed services, prisoners who have served in 9
arts education 106–107, 115, 128
Audio Production Awards 165, 166
Australia:
  community media 26–27
  prison population growth 169
  reconciliation processes 143

B

Barak, G. 121–122
basic skills 106, 107–108
  see also prison education
BBC:
  audio production for 165–166
  changing role of 33, 34–36, 73, 88–94
  and minority audiences 94–95
  prison radio involvement and partnership with PRA 5, 14, 20, 33, 65, 72, 81–99
  prison radio training project 103, 116, 117, 118
  Radio Audiences Team 164

Beaumont, Gustave de 42
bedtime stories 55
Beech, Keith 72
Benjamin, Walter 29
Bentham, Jeremy 44
Berry, Matt 165
Birmingham City University 117
Birt, John 93
Blair, Tony 52, 74
Born, Georgina 33, 35, 82, 88–90, 93
Bottoms, A. 123
Box, Stephen 50
Bragg, Billy 5
Brand, Russell 165
Brecht, Bertolt 29, 33
Brownlee, Ian 52
Byron, Tanya 149, 150, 152, 153, 156–157

C

care leavers 10
Carpentier, Nico 27
Carter and Carter 103
cells, time in 50
Cheliotis, L.K. 124
Christie, Nils 147
citizenship:
  and communication rights 21–22
  and prisoners 27–28
civil death, of prisoners 27
civil society:
  and community media 27
  and prisoners 20
Clements, Paul 106–107
Clinks 66, 70
Coleman, Olivia 165
Collins, Michael 110–111
Comedy School, The 127–129, 137
communication environment of prisons 21–24
community development, and prison radio 144

community media 20, 66
  Australia 26–27
  and civil society 27
contracting out of public services 40, 60
Crawford, A. 151
creative learning 105–111
CSV Media 73, 86, 96, 102, 103, 117
cultural entrepreneurs 75–76
Culture of Control (Garland) 44–45
Cumberbatch, Benedict 165

D

Daily Mail newspaper 122, 126–128, 129–130, 131, 136, 137
Daily Star newspaper 132–133
Davidson, D. 105, 106, 107–108, 112–113, 114, 116–117
Davis, Angela 40, 171
De Medmaecker, Vicky 146, 147
decarceration strategies 171
delinquency 45–46
Department for Work and Pensions 166
developing countries, radio and social change in 25
Di Ronco, A. 138
digitalisation 36
disabilities, people with, and US radio policy 31–32
Discipline and Punish: the Birth of the Prison (Foucault) 43–44
discourse 12–13
Does Prison Work? programme 5
Douglas, Susan J. 23, 25, 26
Douglas, Torin 136
drug education 174
Dubber, Andrew 24–25
Dyke, Greg 93

E

Ear Hustle 172
education *see* prison education
'Education, Training and Employment' pathway, *Reducing Reoffending National Action Plan* 106
Electric Radio Brixton 5–6, 11, 48, 68, 72, 130, 137, 144, 163
emancipation, and adult education 108–109
empowerment, and adult and prison education 108–110
England and Wales:
  prison population growth 40
  prison system crisis 48–56
  privatisation of prisons 40–41
  see also UK
entrepreneurship 60, 74–75, 76, 77
EQUAL funding, European Structural Fund 103
Europe, early development and role of radio in 20, 29
'expert citizen' role 9

F

Face to Face documentary 15, 141–142, 145–146, 148–159
Fairclough, Norman 84–85
Family Man 5, 55
Feeley, M. 52–53
First Nations People, prison population growth 39, 169
Fisher, Mark 128
former prisoners, peer mentoring by 9
Foucault, Michel 12, 21, 43–44, 45, 46
Fry, Stephen 166

G

Garland, David 44–45
Garnier, Edward 133, 134
'Gay on the Inside' 166
Giddens, Anthony 65
Goodman, David 30
governments, and radio 28–32
Gray, Patricia 142–143
Green, D.A. 123–124
Greer, Chris 146–147
Guardian newspaper 122, 128, 129–130, 130–131, 136, 137
Gypsy, Roma and Traveller community 9–10, 148

INDEX

H

Hall, Stuart 12, 45, 51
Hallin, Daniel C. 26
Hardwick, Nick 22
Harrison, Jackie 95–96, 96–97
Hartley, John 33
Hastings, Michael 85, 86
Hendy, David 25–26
Her Majesty's Prison *see* HMP
Her Majesty's Young Offender Institution *see* HMYOI
HMP Birmingham 4–5, 72, 86, 87, 96, 105
HMP Brixton 5–6, 7, 48, 102, 107, 129, 163
   Letters Live broadcast 164–165
   programme production 8–9, 168
HMP Brockhill 105
HMP Hewell 86, 96, 105
HMP Long Lartin 105, 112
HMP Manchester 51
HMP Shrewsbury 116
HMP Styal 8–9, 168
HMP Wandsworth 54
HMP Whitemoor Maximum Security Prison 127
HMP Wormwood Scrubs 51
HMYOI Brinsford 105
HMYOI Swinfen Hall 105
HMPPS (Her Majesty's Prison and Probation Service) 6, 7, 82–83
HMYOI Feltham 3–4, 68
HMYOI Hindley 83
Hood, Stuart 29
Hooper, Roma 4, 12, 66, 67, 69–70, 71, 85, 86, 87, 93–94, 126, 131, 135, 141, 164
Horkheimer, Max 30
Hutton, Will 154–155
HYPE (Hindley Young Persons' Entertainment) 83

I

ICT skills 106
'ideal victim' 147, 152
ImpetusPEF 164
incarceration rates *see* prison population growth
Incite! 62, 64
independents 75–76
indigenous communities, peace and reconciliation processes 143–144
industrial disputes in prisons 51
Inglis, Tom 109–110
Inside at Christmas programme 5
Inside Time 164
internet, access to in prisons 21–22, 24
'Is Prison Obsolete?' conference 63
Israel 171–172

J

Jacka, Elizabeth 90–92
Jail Guitar Doors 5
Jewkes, Yvonne 21–22
Johnston, Helen 21–22
Jones, Mick 5

K

key skills 106, 107–108
   see also prison education
Khan, Javed 145–146
Kirkpatrick, Bill 31–32
Kivel, Paul 63–64
Knight, Victoria 23, 24

L

Lacey, Nicola 48
'lags' 132–133
language skills 106
Leadbeater, Charles 74–75, 76
Letters Live broadcast 164–165
Lewis, Peter 22
Lie, Rico 27
listener engagement and participation 8, 20, 24, 174
literacy 105, 106
Loach, Ken 175
London Probation Trust 166
Longford Lecture 2017 168, 175
Longford Prize 165, 168

LSC (Learning and Skills Council) 102
OLASS (Offender Learning and Skills Service) 103

M

Maguire, Phil 5, 12, 22, 71–72, 72–73, 74, 86, 87–88, 89, 94, 101, 126, 135, 136–137, 141, 164
Making Waves Behind Bars CD 5, 39
managerialism 40, 66, 92–93
Māori people, Aotearoa New Zealand 169
Mason, Paul 13, 124–125, 132–133
McCarthy, Jules 12, 104, 112–114, 115–117
McDowell, Paul 12, 48, 107, 129, 130
Meadows, M. 26–27
media:
  context 2
  deregulation 34–35, 36
  see also news media
Ministry of Justice 5, 6, 7, 82, 96, 98
  press office 135, 136
minority audiences, and the BBC 94–95
mobile telephones, access to in prisons 21
Morison, John 66
'mugging,' social construction of 45
Munshi, S. 63, 64

N

national identity, and radio 29
Navajo Nation, peacemaking process 143–144
neoliberalism 26, 40, 41, 45, 46, 47, 51, 63, 170
New Labour 51–52, 65, 74–75, 84, 93, 142–143
New Penology theory 52–53
New Public Management 93
New York International Radio Awards 166
New Zealand, prison population growth 169

news media:
  and PRA (Prison Radio Association) 14–15, 121–122, 126–139
  and prisons 122–125
  see also media
'Newsmaking Criminology' theory 121–122
newspapers:
  access to in prisons 21
  see also news media
NOMS (National Offender Management Service) 5, 6, 87
non-profit industrial complex 62, 63–64
non-profit sector 14, 59, 61–67, 76
NPR (National Prison Radio) 1–2, 7, 11, 41–42, 163–164
  activities and ethos 53–54, 56
  background and early development 6–10
  as institutional and alternative media 28
  listener engagement 8, 174
  Longford Lecture 2017 168, 175
  prison context 48–56
  programming 7, 8–9
numeracy 106

O

Oakley, K. 75, 76
Open Road programme 9–10
Outside In programme 9

P

panopticon 44, 54
partnerships 14
  discursive repositioning of under neoliberalism 83–84
  PRA/BBC 20, 33, 35–36, 65, 72, 81–99
  PRA/Ministry of Justice 82, 96, 98
  PRA's partnership way of working 82–83, 84–85, 98–99
Peacock Report 1984 35
peer mentoring, by former prisoners 9

INDEX

people of colour, prison population growth 39
Phillips, Andrew 85
podcasts 24
political and policy context 61–67
Porridge programme 7
power, and prisons 42–47
  prison education 110–111
PRA (Prison Radio Association) 1–2, 11, 42
  activities and ethos 56–57, 101–102, 167, 173
  background and early development 3–6
  core aim of 19, 173
  evaluation strategy 164
  Face to Face documentary 15, 141–142, 145–146, 148–159
  independence of 28–29, 37, 54, 97–98
  media strategy 135–137, 158
  and news media 14–15, 121–139, 158
  partnership way of working 82–83, 84–85, 98–99
  partnership with BBC 20, 33, 35–36, 65, 72, 81–99
  partnership with Ministry of Justice 82, 96, 98
  prison radio training project 101–105, 112, 117, 118–119
  relationship with prisoners 83
  reputational risk 126–135
  Straightline 167–168
  tenth anniversary 164–165
  third sector context 65–66
  volunteerism and social activism 70
PRA Impact Snapshot 164
PRA Productions 165–166
prison context 2–3, 13, 39–42
  and power 42–47
  UK 47, 48–57
prison education 14, 55, 109–110
  arts education 106–107, 115, 128
  Collins' critique of 110–111
  context and creative learning 105–111
  see also prison radio training project

prison industrial complex 41, 64, 170–171
prison overcrowding, England and Wales 49, 170
prison population growth 39–40, 51, 167, 168–169, 170–171
prison radio 11
  community development function of 144
  contemporary significance of 168–172
  international developments 171–172
  listener engagement 20
  motivation of participants 59–60
  non-profit sector context 64–65
  role in connecting prisoners with civil society 20
  volunteerism and social activism 69, 71
  see also NPR (National Prison Radio); PRA (Prison Radio Association)
Prison Radio International 172
prison radio training project 101–105, 118–119
  and creative learning 105–111
  project design and delivery 111–118
Prison Reform Trust 170
prisoners:
  and citizenship 27–28, 32
  and civil society 20
  voice of 172–176
prisons:
  communication environment of 21–24
  negative impact of 45
  and news media 122–125
  violence in 3–4, 49–50, 170
  volunteers and voluntary agencies in 66–67, 69–70
privatisation:
  of prisons 40–41
  of social welfare 62–63
problem solving skills 106
profit, and punishment 41
PSB (public service broadcasting) 20, 32–36, 82

evolution and change in 81, 90–91, 94–98
public realm, demise of 154–155
punishment 40, 41

R

radical democracy 28, 91
radio:
  context 13
  early development and role of 29–32
  and social change 25
  and state government 28–32
  transformation of 2, 24–25
  transformative power of 13, 19, 22–23, 30–31
  see also prison radio
Radio Academy 'Indie of the Year' award 166
Radio Academy 'Station of the Year' awards 165
radio democracy 24–28
Radio Feltham 11, 48, 61, 68, 72, 73, 83, 85, 86
Radio Focus 171–172
Radio Fri 172
Radio Wanno 54
RAJAR (Radio Joint Audiences Research) 164
Reagan, Ronald 45
reconciliation processes 143–144
  see also restorative justice
Reducing Reoffending National Action Plan 106
rehabilitation, and prison radio 55
reintegration models 9
reoffending 167
  reduction of 7, 9, 19
Request Show, The programme 8
research overview 10–15
respect, in restorative justice 154, 155–156
restorative justice 142–147, 153–154, 156
  Face to Face documentary 15, 141–142, 145–146, 148–159
Restorative Justice Council 145–146

Revolution Will Not Be Funded, The (Incite!) 62, 64
Robinson, Mark 4, 12, 69, 71
Rodriguez, Clemencia 28
Roll Call programme 9
Rose d'Or award 166
Rwanda 143
Ryan, Mick 41

S

Sabbagh, Dan 136
Safe Ground 55, 168
Safe programme 10
Samaritans 166
San Quentin State Prison, California 172
Scannell, P. 33–34, 36
self-harm in prisons 50
  HMYOI Feltham 4, 68
  NPR (National Prison Radio) response to 54
Seppings, Claire 9
Servaes, Jan 27
Sheffield Hallam University Centre for Community Justice 102–103
Sim, Joe 4, 51, 123
Simon, J. 52–53
Sisters Inside 63
Snow, Jon 175
social activism 14, 59, 60, 61, 67, 68–69, 70, 71–72, 77
social enterprise and entrepreneurship 14, 59, 60
social welfare, privatisation of 62–63
Sokolowski, Wojciech 70–71
Solomon, E. 125, 138
Sony Radio Academy Awards 7, 130, 136–137, 165
Sound Women programme 9
South Africa 143
Sparks, R. 125, 139
Spurr, Michael 6–7
Story Book Dads 55
Story Book Mums 55
Straightline 167–168
Strang, Heather 151

INDEX

Straw, Jack 127–128, 128–129, 133, 134
street crime, social construction of 45
Strong, Mark 165
suicides in prisons 49–50
  HMYOI Feltham 4, 68, 69, 70
  NPR (National Prison Radio) response to 54
Sullivan, Dennis 143–144
Sun, The newspaper 122, 127, 128, 131–132, 133, 135, 137
Sweden 172

T

'Takeover Days' 9
Telegraph, The (newspaper) 128
television, access to in prisons 21, 23
Tempest, Kate 165
Thatcher, Margaret 34–35, 45, 51
third sector 60–61, 65–66
Third Sector 'Charity of the Year' Award 164
Third Sector Excellence Awards 141, 145
Third Way 65, 67, 77
Thompson, Mark 93
Tifft, Larry 143–144
Tilley, Kieron 12, 71–72, 72–74, 85–86, 87–88, 89, 94, 101–102, 132
Times, The newspaper 136, 137
Tocqueville, Alexis de 42

U

UK:
  prison context 3, 47, 48–57
  see also England and Wales
understaffing in prisons 50, 170
US:
  early development and role of radio 20, 23, 29, 31–32
  prison population growth 39, 40, 169
  prison radio 172

V

Victim Support:
  Face to Face documentary 15, 141–142, 145–146, 148–159
victims of crime:
  Face to Face documentary 15, 141–142, 145–146, 148–159
  'ideal victim' 147, 152
  restorative justice 142–147
  victim role 154–155
  voice and perspective of 146–147
violence in prisons 3–4, 49–50, 170
Voluntary Sector Co-ordinator for the Prison Service 66
volunteerism 14, 59, 60, 61, 66, 68–69, 69–71, 77
volunteers and voluntary agencies in prisons 66–67, 69–70

W

Wacquant, Loïc 2–3, 4, 46–47, 51, 138, 170
Walklate, Sandra 154–155
Waltz, Mitzi 2, 26
Ward, Tony 41
Weinberg, Charlotte 168
Wessels, Bridgette 95–96, 96–97
West Midlands project 5, 10, 14, 72, 81, 85, 86, 94, 102, 103, 111, 117, 118
Wilkie, Andrew 12, 71–72, 144, 163, 174
Wilkinson, K. 105, 106, 107–108, 112–113, 114, 116–117
Williams, Zoe 136
Willse, C. 63, 64
Wilson, John 70
women prisoners 63
  incarceration rates 8
  prison population growth 39
  self-harm/suicides in prisons 50
working together skills 106